Across the Rivers of Memory

THE AZRIELI SERIES OF HOLOCAUST SURVIVOR MEMOIRS:
PUBLISHED TITLES

ENGLISH TITLES

Across the Rivers of Memory
Felicia (Steigman) Carmelly

FIRST EDITION
Copyright © 2015 The Azrieli Foundation and others

THE AZRIELI FOUNDATION
www.azrielifoundation.org

Cover and book design by Mark Goldstein
Endpaper maps by Martin Gilbert
Map on page xxxiii by François Blanc

LIBRARY AND ARCHIVES CANADA CATALOGUING IN PUBLICATION

Carmelly, Felicia Steigman, 1931–, author
    Across the rivers of memory / Felicia (Steigman) Carmelly.

(Azrieli series of Holocaust survivor memoirs. Series 7)
Includes index.
ISBN 978-1-897470-54-1 (paperback)

1. Carmelly, Felicia Steigman, 1931–. 2. Holocaust, Jewish (1939–1945) – Romania – Personal narratives. 3. Transnistria (Ukraine : Territory under German and Romanian occupation, 1941–1944). 4. Holocaust survivors – Canada – Biography. I. Azrieli Foundation, issuing body II. Title. III. Series: Azrieli series of Holocaust survivor memoirs. Series 7

DS135.R7C365 2015   940.53'1809498   C2015-905605-5

PRINTED IN CANADA

The Azrieli Series of Holocaust Survivor Memoirs

Naomi Azrieli, Publisher

Jody Spiegel, Program Director
Arielle Berger, Managing Editor
Elizabeth Lasserre, Senior Editor, French-Language Editions
Farla Klaiman, Editor
Elin Beaumont, Senior Educational Outreach and Events Coordinator
Catherine Person, Educational Outreach and Events Coordinator,
    Quebec and French Canada
Marc-Olivier Cloutier, Educational Outreach and Events Assistant,
    Quebec and French Canada
Tim MacKay, Digital Platform Manager
Elizabeth Banks, Digital Asset and Archive Curator
Susan Roitman, Office Manager (Toronto)
Mary Mellas, Executive Assistant and Human Resources (Montreal)

Mark Goldstein, Art Director
François Blanc, Cartographer
Bruno Paradis, Layout, French-language editions

Contents

Series Preface:
In their own words. . .

In telling these stories, the writers have liberated themselves. For so many years we did not speak about it, even when we became free people living in a free society. Now, when at last we are writing about what happened to us in this dark period of history, knowing that our stories will be read and live on, it is possible for us to feel truly free. These unique historical documents put a face on what was lost, and allow readers to grasp the enormity of what happened to six million Jews – one story at a time.

> David J. Azrieli, C.M., C.Q., M.Arch
> Holocaust survivor and founder, The Azrieli Foundation

Since the end of World War II, over 30,000 Jewish Holocaust survivors have immigrated to Canada. Who they are, where they came from, what they experienced and how they built new lives for themselves and their families are important parts of our Canadian heritage. The Azrieli Foundation's Holocaust Survivor Memoirs Program was established to preserve and share the memoirs written by those who survived the twentieth-century Nazi genocide of the Jews of Europe and later made their way to Canada. The program is guided by the conviction that each survivor of the Holocaust has a remarkable story to tell, and that such stories play an important role in education about tolerance and diversity.

Millions of individual stories are lost to us forever. By preserving the stories written by survivors and making them widely available to a broad audience, the Azrieli Foundation's Holocaust Survivor Memoirs Program seeks to sustain the memory of all those who perished at the hands of hatred, abetted by indifference and apathy. The personal accounts of those who survived against all odds are as different as the people who wrote them, but all demonstrate the courage, strength, wit and luck that it took to prevail and survive in such terrible adversity. The memoirs are also moving tributes to people – strangers and friends – who risked their lives to help others, and who, through acts of kindness and decency in the darkest of moments, frequently helped the persecuted maintain faith in humanity and courage to endure. These accounts offer inspiration to all, as does the survivors' desire to share their experiences so that new generations can learn from them.

The Holocaust Survivor Memoirs Program collects, archives and publishes these distinctive records and the print editions are available free of charge to educational institutions and Holocaust-education programs across Canada. They are also available for sale to the general public at bookstores. All revenues to the Azrieli Foundation from the sales of the Azrieli Series of Holocaust Survivor Memoirs go toward the publishing and educational work of the memoirs program.

The Azrieli Foundation would like to express appreciation to the following people for their invaluable efforts in producing this book: Doris Bergen, Sherry Dodson (Maracle Press), Barbara Kamieński, Therese Parent, and Margie Wolfe and Emma Rodgers of Second Story Press.

About the Glossary

The following memoir contains a number of terms, concepts and historical references that may be unfamiliar to the reader. For information on major organizations; significant historical events and people; geographical locations; religious and cultural terms; and foreign-language words and expressions that will help give context and background to the events described in the text, please see the glossary beginning on page 121.

Introduction

Felicia Carmelly's life story hurls the reader into a tumultuous history and experience of places, societies and people of extraordinary variety. From beautiful Dorna, a town in southern Bukovina, to the deadly sites of Transnistria, to post-war Romania, then Israel and, finally, contemporary Canada, these pages illuminate a fascinating history and offer insight into myriad subjects. This history is palpable – alive with sounds, smells and colours, filled with details that even trained historians may find new.

At the same time, *Across the Rivers of Memory* is the testimony of a Holocaust survivor, and nothing makes that clearer than the author's motivation to write it. Felicia Carmelly felt compelled to fill the gaps in her family history for her younger relatives and saw herself as responsible for keeping alive the memory of Jewish suffering in Transnistria. In doing the latter, Ms. Carmelly has gone far and beyond this memoir. As early as 1972, during a visit to Romania (as a Canadian citizen), she took the initiative to address officials from the Ministry of Education, expressing the need to teach the Holocaust in Romania's secondary schools. In 1994, Felicia Carmelly founded the Transnistria Survivors' Association in Canada and became its president. Between 1995 and 1997 she worked on a monumental project – a publication entitled *Shattered! 50 Years of Silence: History and Voices of the Tragedy in Romania and Transnistria.* The volume includes a detailed history of Transnistria, together with some official documents of the era and personal testimonies of Holocaust survivors. Felicia reflects on the uncanny feeling she had that producing this anthology, which sought to bear witness and expose the horrors of Transnistria to the world at large, was, in fact, the meaning of her life and the purpose of her survival.

It is only in the past few decades that the Holocaust in Eastern Europe has become a subject of intense scrutiny, and earlier societal reactions to the Holocaust underline the complex political considerations behind its silencing. Initially, as in other post-war European countries, gentiles' fears of punishment for complicity in crimes, as well as competing victimhoods, were among the reasons for the overwhelming silence about the Holocaust. States, in their effort to consolidate societies torn apart by war, instead built legitimacy through narratives of national heroism and martyrdom; they were not keen to complicate these unambiguous histories with accounts that focused specifically on the destruction of Jewish communities.

This avoidance, accompanied by the failure of post-war East European regimes to officially recognize the extent of Jewish suffering, inflicted serious emotional pain on Holocaust survivors. As Felicia notes in her memoir, the particular handling of the history of the Holocaust by the Romanian and Soviet regimes after World War II was "the ultimate betrayal." Yet, even after the fall of communism this situation did not show signs of rapid improvement. During the 1990s most of Eastern Europe, Romania included, went through an acute phase of nationalism, marked by a staunch refusal to admit the criminal behaviour of pre-war and World War II regimes. Sometimes, this included blunt Holocaust denial and accusations that Jews themselves attracted the murderous brunt of their country's authorities.[1]

---

1 For example, some historians and public intellectuals have accused the Jewish community of collaboration with Soviet authorities in the summer of 1940, and

For example, after 1989, Ion Antonescu – the Romanian dictator responsible for the destruction of over 250,000 Jews – was acclaimed as a national hero by the Romanian public, as the one who fought the Soviet Union to liberate Bessarabia. It was not until 2005, after an international outcry caused by the president of Romania's Holocaust denial, that Romania created a committee to document crimes committed by Romanian authorities during the war, officially recognizing its responsibility in perpetrating the Holocaust.

～

Felicia (née Steigman) Carmelly was born in 1931 in the town of Vatra Dornei (Dorna), Bukovina, which was part of eastern Romania at the time. She was the only daughter of Laura (Lipzia) and Isaac (Yitzhak) Steigman, both natives of Dorna. The family's cultural and political references were shaped by the particularities of the Bukovinian milieu. Historically part of the Principality of Moldavia, the territory of Bukovina was annexed by the Habsburg Monarchy after the 1775 partition of the Principality of Moldavia between the Austrian and Ottoman Empires. During the nineteenth century, the Austrian Empire introduced policies that encouraged an influx of numerous immigrants, aiming to boost the region's economy. Among the newcomers were many Germans, Poles, Jews, Hungarians, Ukrainians and Romanians.

During the subsequent century, Habsburg Bukovina became known as "the most multinational crown-land." The Jews in the Habsburg Empire appreciated the regime's toleration of all nationalities and its commitment to the idea of *Rechtsstaat,* a concept of justice that became particularly prominent during the second half of the nineteenth century. Yet, the regime's greater tolerance had differ-

––––––––––––––––––

argue that the subsequent genocidal policies under Antonescu were collective "punishment" for "treacherous" behaviour.

ing impacts on the various ethnic groups and nations inhabiting the empire: Ukrainians and Romanians, for example, experienced growing national aspirations and increasingly vied against each other and the imperial centre, while a growing sense of loyalty was developing among its Jewish population.

This loyalty is usually explained by the fact that Austrian policy offered social and economic opportunities for Jews that were unmatched in most neighbouring countries. Austrian Bukovina Jews enjoyed not only social and economic prominence, but also political importance. Czernowitz, for example, had several Jewish mayors during the last two decades of Austrian rule. The Empire also offered Jews the possibility to retain their Jewish identity (either religious or secular), while simultaneously offering an alternative of assimilating into the dominant German culture. Given these circumstances, and the severe restrictions on Jewish communities that existed in other European countries, broad Jewish support for the Austrian Empire is not surprising. As Alfred Rieber astutely noted, "It is only a slightly tarnished truism that of all the peoples of the Habsburg Monarchy the Jews were the most Kaisertreu [loyal to the Emperor]."[2]

With the collapse of Austro-Hungary in 1918, Romania took over Bukovina, a change that was recognized internationally by the Treaty of Saint-Germain (1919). Romania emerged from World War I significantly enlarged both geographically and demographically, incorporating Bukovina from Austria, Transylvania from Hungary, and Bessarabia from Russia. The nineteenth-century dream of many Romanian intellectuals – of uniting all ethnic Romanians and their "historic" territories into one state – finally seemed to come to life. At the same time, the enlarged state of Greater Romania encompassed new demographic realities and was less homogeneous than before.

---

2   Alfred J. Rieber, *The Struggle for the Eurasian Borderlands. From the Rise of Early Modern Empires to the End of the First World War* (Cambridge: Cambridge University Press, 2014), p. 88.

Of the three provinces newly incorporated in Romania, Bukovina was the least ethnically Romanian. Its northern part was heavily populated by Ukrainians, who outnumbered the area's Romanians. In 1910, Ukrainians were the primary ethnic group (38.4 per cent), followed by Romanians (34.4 per cent), Jews (12 per cent), and Germans (9.3 per cent).[3]

The new post-World War I demographic reality heightened Romania's sense of vulnerability in the face of its revisionist neighbours – the Soviet Union, Hungary and Bulgaria.[4] During the interwar period, the Romanian state embarked on a modernization project that was nationalist in character. Similar to many other nationalist regimes from this period, the Romanian state's primary goal was to construct a state that would ensure the flourishing and development of "its own" people – ethnic Romanians – and the state's energy had to be channelled to this ultimate aspiration. The role of minorities in this context was highly problematic. By design, these minorities were imagined as disloyal, deemed threatening to the stability of the Romanian state, and these suspicions became especially magnified when referring to minorities residing in contested border territories, such as Bukovina.

By 1930, the ethnic makeup of Bukovina's populace changed significantly, yet it was still far removed from the Romanian nationalists' ideal. A census from that year showed that Romanians comprised 44.5 per cent; Ukrainians 29.1 per cent; Jews 10.8 per cent, and Germans 8.9 per cent. More broadly, according to the Romanian nationalist design, in Bukovina a Romanianization process aimed to wipe out the legacy of previous Austrian policies, which the Romanian historian Ion Nistor contemptuously called "Bukovinism" and "homo bukovinensis." According to many leading Romanian intellectuals at

---

3   Irina Livezeanu, *Cultural Politics in Greater Romania: Regionalism, Nation Building and Ethnic Struggle, 1918–1930* (Ithaca: Cornell University Press, 1995), p. 49.

4   Romania annexed Southern Dobruja from Bulgaria after the Second Balkan War, in 1913.

the time, the careless mixing of the ethnic groups and the use of German as a lingua franca had to stop, while the "Romanian spirit" had
to be instilled in the masses. As one scholar of Romania observed,
since Bukovina's Jews had what Romanians coveted most – education and urban status – it was especially important to unseat Jews as
a symbol of Romanian achievement.[5]

That same 1930 census counted 9,826 people residing in Dorna,
including 1,747 Jews, or 17.8 per cent of the population.[6] The long-
standing cultural legacies of the previous regime were still visible to
the Romanian authorities at that time: about 19 per cent of the Jews
of Dorna identified their mother tongue as "other than Yiddish," and
these were Jews who primarily spoke German.[7]

The Steigman family illustrates the symbiosis of the Bukovinian
Jews' acculturation into the dominant Austro-Hungarian culture,
while preserving a traditional Jewish approach to social and religious
life. Felicia, for example, identified her native language as "Austrian
German" and expressed particular pride in Bukovinian Jews for belonging to the realm of German culture. As she wrote, this was a spirit
that could have been deciphered from the "proud snobbishness about
our Germanic-Austrian traits," which made the Bukovinian Jews feel
superior to the Jews from other parts of Romania.

Life in interwar Dorna (1918–1939) was part of the microcosm of
interwar Jewish life in Bukovina and Eastern Europe more broadly,
where children were expected to marry according to their parents'
wishes and live in the same house with their parents after marriage.
Typical of this situation, Felicia describes how her mother was asked
to marry not the man she loved, but a man who was in love with her

---

5   Livezeanu, p. 78.

6   Ed. Sabin Manuilă, *Recesământul general al populației române. Din 29 decemvrie
    1930*, Volumul II Neam, limbă maternă, religie (București: Imprimeria nationala,
    1938), p. XL–XLI.

7   Ibid. p.XXVI

(Yitzhak, Felicia's future father), who was financially better off and could support the dowry for her two other sisters. The newly married couple moved into Yizhak's parents' house and made their living in their family business, running haberdashery stores. The clothing business, along with lumber and shoemaking, were typical Jewish businesses in the area. The patterns of Jewish life in Dorna were identical to those in other areas of Eastern Europe, although Dorna was also a spa town. This last detail gave the town an additional cosmopolitan aura, featuring graceful summer homes, numerous cafes, a casino and abundant tourists leisurely strolling in its grand park.

Being born in a middle-class family, surrounded by the care and love of her extended family, Felicia grew up in the interwar period believing that "life was easygoing and we had everything we needed." The family took special pride in their fine house, which Felicia notes had running water – a rare luxury at the time. When free of daily work and other duties, the Steigmans visited friends, hosted parties, went to movies and took strolls in Dorna's beautiful park. Antisemitism did not seem to seriously affect Felicia's earlier life. "It was not that antisemitism did not exist in Romania. It was just that it would come and go with such frequency and familiarity that Jews learned how to cope with it." However, while the protective shell of Felicia's extended family and the cosmopolitan life of Dorna may have softened Felicia's perceptions of antisemitism in Romania, she was not spared its direct brunt when a newly antisemitic regime came to power. In the fall of 1940, Felicia, a pupil in Grade 3, was expelled from school along with other Jewish children.

The antisemitic dispositions of Romanian society during the interwar era were not particularly "unique" or extraordinary in the context of Eastern Europe at the time. In fact, there had been a centuries-long tradition of antisemitism among the Romanian intelligentsia and local establishment. Despite Romania's promising legal beginnings in 1919, many sources attest to the reality of Jewish discrimination throughout state and society during the interwar years. Formally equal in rights, in practice all Romanian Jews remained second-class citizens: positions within the core of the state power structure, such as the army, police, judiciary and other powerful institutions, remained clearly unattainable for the Jewish minority, and obstacles and restrictions were placed in the way of those seeking higher education.

Moreover, Romanian state institutions were directly responsible for antisemitism's proliferation by interpreting many of Romania's social, economic and political dysfunctions as primarily the result of Jewish exploitation. Documents produced by the security organs reveal an entrenched perception of the Jews as a threat to the Romanian state. Scholar Raphael Vago has noted that the results of these policies and approaches led Jews to develop a kind of a siege mentality.[8] In the 1930s in the nationalistic and xenophobic Greater Romania, traditional hostility toward Jews moved to the forefront of political and intellectual life. Antisemitism featured regularly in the mainstream press, satirical publications and student rallies, while also being advanced by popular political parties such as the LANC (Liga Apărării Național Creștine, the National-Christian Defense League) and Iron Guard, which treated antisemitism as a philosophic and aesthetic creed.[9]

In December 1937, a newly formed government effectively legalized antisemitism, while bands of right-wing activists launched a wave of vandalism in Jewish districts, looting and destroying Jewish property. The antisemitic hysteria intensified in the summer of 1940, after the Soviet Union's ultimatum to Romania and the Soviet occupation of Northern Bukovina and Bessarabia. Humiliated by successful

8 Raphael Vago, "Romanian Jewry During the Interwar Period," in *The Tragedy of Romanian Jewry*, ed. Randolph L. Braham (New York: Columbia University Press, 1994), 32.

9 On Romanian antisemitism in interwar period see Leon Volovici, *Nationalist Ideology and Antisemitism: The Case of Romanian Intellectuals in the 1930s* (Oxford: Pergamon Press, 1991).

Soviet aggression and infuriated by the welcoming of Soviet authorities by parts of Romania's population, Romanian officials identified Jews as the ultimate enemy of the Romanian people. A number of massacres of Jews accompanied Romania's military withdrawal at the time. These massacres were typically carried out by Romanian soldiers, with the support of local Romanian and Ukrainian gentiles.

About one year later, in the summer of 1941, after Romania started its military campaign against the Soviet Union in alliance with Nazi Germany, the unfolding policy of assault towards the Jewish population turned into an organized murderous policy of "terrain cleansing" in Bessarabia, Bukovina and Transnistria, clearly surpassing even the wildest dreams of the most incorrigible Romanian antisemites. Romanian gendarmes began massacring Jews from the rural areas of Bukovina and Bessarabia immediately upon arriving in those territories. Thousands of Jews were killed within weeks. The Jews from towns and cities, as well as those few who managed to survive the first wave of atrocities, were locked for weeks and months in makeshift camps and ghettos and later deported to camps in eastern Transnistria where they were killed or imprisoned in such conditions that most did not survive to see the end of the war. Altogether, between 154,000 and 170,000 Jews of Bukovina, Bessarabia and the Dorohoi county were deported to Transnistria, forced to walk hundreds of kilometres, some dying en route.[10] Transnistria, a part of occupied Ukraine under Romanian administration, became an enormous killing field both for Jews deported from Romania as well as for local Ukrainian Jews. The Jews who originated from Transnistria received similar, brutal treatment. Systematic killings, starvation and diseases took the lives of an estimated 280,000 to 380,000 Romanian and Ukrainian Jews.

Romania's increasing assault on its Jewry is aptly illustrated by

10 Eds. Tuvia Friling et al., *International Commission on the Holocaust in Romania: Final Report* (Iași: Polirom, 2005), p. 176.

Felicia's description of the changes she observed taking place in Dorna in 1940–1941. Curfews, prohibition of intermarriage, bans on the sale of alcohol, prohibition of gathering in synagogues, the compulsory yellow star – all of these were new realities for Dorna's Jewish population. Relationships with gentiles, which Felicia had previously characterized as friendly, entered a new phase of distancing from each other. This was a period when Felicia's parents went into a "shushing mode," when discussing current events. Even Jewish children's games demonstrate perceptions of an aggravated political situation in 1940–1941, while simultaneously illustrating the social and gender stereotypes dominant in middle-class Bukovinian Jewish families. For example, Felicia played the "famous wives" game, where children pretended to be the Romanian King's wife; Marshal Antonescu's wife – who was supposed to be "really mean"; and the wife of Hitler.

Given that the Holocaust in Transnistria is a relatively new area of study, Felicia's testimony is of utmost importance. Unlike the deportations from the Dorohoi county and Bessarabia, the deportation of Jews from southern Bukovina remains under-researched. Documents produced by the Romanian officials from that period indicate that 21,229 Jews from southern Bukovina were deported to Transnistria in 1941 and 1942. During those deportations, Jews were allowed to take with them only few personal effects. On their marches to various locations in Transnistria, Jews were forced to walk on foot for days or sometimes weeks without adequate supplies of food and water. Those who could not keep pace were shot by Romanian soldiers, or left behind to die in the middle of the road. Felicia's account exemplifies the appalling scenes witnessed on the roads of Transnistria: "The roads were lined with fresh cadavers bloated from hunger or partially ripped open by animals. These were the victims of previous convoys of deportees."

The Steigman family's agonizing road to Shargorod broadly mirrors the experience of other southern Bukovinian Jews. Their deportation started with the family locked into a cattle car and driven for days before arriving in the city of Ataki. They were next moved across the Dniester River by barge, spent a few days in the town of Mogilev, and then marched for three more days by foot until reaching the town of Shargorod, where the family was imprisoned in the local ghetto. Felicia's description of their departure from her native town and the travel inside the cattle car offers one of the most gripping scenes of her memoir. The ten-year-old girl's senses carefully examine and portray the crowd at the train station, with all their accompanying sounds and smells, as well as the angst absorbing the people around her inside the train. As with many other Holocaust survivors' memoirs, Felicia's testimony attests both to humanity's solidarity as well as to the brutal decomposition of society that occurs when placed in inhuman conditions.

Upon arrival at their final Transnistria destination, Jewish deportees were imprisoned in unimaginable conditions, such as crowded ghettos, barns, pig stalls, forests and open fields.[11] Hunger became overwhelming, as deportees were incarcerated for years without any means of subsistence. In the majority of cases, the authorities did not feed the Jews at all; when they did provide food, it was either meagre or inedible or both.[12]

Forcibly isolated from the rest of society, Jews had to make extraordinary efforts to stay alive. Many of the valuables that the deportees had possessed were confiscated at the time of their arrest, or were later stolen by guards and locals during deportation. The few things that Jews managed to hide were insufficient to support their families in Transnistria during their long period of detention. Whenever Jews managed to survive the deportation marches and the har-

---

11 For a detailed description of Jewish life in Transnistria between 1941 and 1944, see Jean Ancel, *Transnistria* (Tel Aviv: Tel Aviv University Press, 2003), vol. 1.

12 In Vapniarka camp, for example, the inmates had to eat field peas, which caused paralysis in the legs (interview with Ana Bughici, Y VA, VT/2413; Ihiel Benditer, *Vapniarca* [Tel Aviv: Anais Ltd., 1995]).

rowing conditions of the camps in Transnistria, it was almost always thanks to interactions with the local inhabitants. In the Shargorod ghetto, the Steigman family was sheltered by a Jewish family who had only a kitchen and two rooms. They offered to shelter eighteen more people, and were even prepared to share their scant resources, whenever available.

Felicia Carmelly's memoir provides a window into daily life in Shargorod – the relationships between deportees and their interactions with local Jews and gentiles; methods of survival; and the liberation of the ghetto. Felicia was lucky to be among those who survived until their liberation in 1944; moreover, she survived together with her parents, maternal grandmother and a few relatives. At the same time, a staggering thirty-six members of her family, including her paternal grandparents, perished in Transnistria.

Felicia and her family faced profound, continuous suffering, and when the Steigman family arrived back in Romania in late 1945, they had effectively returned to a different country. The family's post-war efforts to resume their lives are broadly embedded into the grander canvas of the post-war transformations in Romania. With the support of the Soviet occupation forces, a communist regime was established. Felicia candidly admits to being enthralled with communist ideology. For her, as well as for the majority of her friends, all members of a communist youth association, communism at that time was "God's gift to the universe; with its lofty ideals of equality, fraternity and liberty, as in the French Revolution." It was through a network of communist organizations that Felicia became involved in the reconstruction of the Dorna community, focusing particularly on the opening of a local high school.

Felicia's involvement with communist ideology was not uncommon. While most East European Jews were not supporters of communism, communism's embrace by parts of the Jewish population is a complicated story, with deep roots in the history of turbulent Jewish-gentile relations and the appeal of an egalitarian ideology for oppressed minorities. For centuries, most religions and nationalist ideologies singled out Jews as the "other," denying them a dignified and culturally Jewish path of belonging to a greater social body. The ideology of communism promised to promote equality for representatives of all ethnic groups, including Jews. The Soviet Union, while making an effort to guard its most hideous truths – such as famines and Stalinist mass purges – was trumpeting its successes in building the "friendship of peoples," where Jews were set to strive and flourish.

Jews of Romania during the interwar era, mindful of their continuously deteriorating condition, closely watched the radically different changes occurring across the country's eastern border. As one historian suitably put it, the mere fact that the first leader of the Communist Party of the Moldavian Autonomous Soviet Socialist Republic (created in 1924 as part of the Ukrainian SSR) was a Jewish person, "speaks volumes" about the difference between the status of Jews inside the Soviet Union, compared to the situation of Jews inside Romania.[13] In the 1920s and 1930s, it was evident to any astute observer that Jews were in highly visible positions within the Soviet army, security apparatus, government, institutions of higher education and many other functions of power and prestige within the USSR, a situation that was not the case in Greater Romania. Coupled with the fact that many Holocaust survivors were liberated by the Soviet army, some Jews in the immediate post-war period chose to believe that, despite the multiple shortages and abuses of the Soviet state, communism was the only ideology able to ensure the basis for equal treatment inside a gentile society.

Like most East European leftist intellectuals, Felicia's idealization of communism was crushed by the realities of the regimes built with-

---

13 Dmitry Tartakovsky, *Parallel Ruptures: Jews of Bessarabia and Transnistria between Romanian Nationalism and Soviet Communism, 1918–1940* (PhD dissertation, University of Illinois at Urbana-Champaign, 2009), p. 233–234.

in Soviet satellite countries after the war. Felicia's involvement with the "real world," and the official lies she was exposed to, ultimately led her to conclude that communism was not, in fact, a better system for the entire population. Felicia came to understand that communism was "a good system only for those who were in the upper echelons of the Communist Party" – a conclusion shared by many others who had earlier been seduced by a doctrine that promised to address the needs and suffering of others. This disenchantment only grew with time and, together with other factors, eventually contributed to her decision to leave Romania and establish a new life in a new homeland.

Felicia's disillusionment with communism had enduring effects on her evaluation of her life's trajectory. She remains riddled by a deep sense of guilt and questions whether leaving Romania a decade earlier would have meant her parents successfully adjusting to their new society. Implicitly, she also questions whether her relationship with her parents would have evolved differently.

In documenting her family's emigration, Felicia contributes to the topic of Jewish emigration from Romania more broadly. At the closure of World War II, slightly more than 350,000 Jews were living in Romania. After the creation of the state of Israel in 1948 and its opening to Jews from the diaspora, the Romanian government suddenly became aware of "valuable" citizens it held inside the country. As Radu Ioanid demonstrates in his superbly researched book *The Ransom of the Jews*, Romania and Israel reached an agreement, implemented by the countries' secret intelligence services, which was nothing less than "ransoming Jews." In a highly secretive operation, which remained hidden for decades, the Israeli government supplied a steady flow of cash (about $3,000 per person) for exit visas provided by Romania to its Jewish citizens, allowing them to emigrate to Israel and the United States.

While these arrangements were being negotiated at the highest political levels, Jewish people themselves were going through a nightmare in their attempt to leave. In order to emigrate, Romanian Jews usually had to apply to their local authorities, and whether permission was granted has been described as completely random. Jews had to wait without any clear perspective in sight, while the Romanian state simultaneously categorized and treated them as an "enemy of the State" for wanting to leave. The latter status meant being discharged from any previously held positions and a broader ostracism of the applicant within society.

Across the Rivers of Memory stands as a monument to any first generation of immigrants, regardless of from where and to which destination they might have emigrated. Readers cannot help but empathize with the tremendous tension of being uprooted and transplanted into new lands, multiple times, without language skills, homes, jobs and social networks. Felicia's family story indicates that, despite Israel's unparalleled appeal for Jews, constructing a new life there was not easily manageable for those who took the difficult path of emigration. Felicia's parents were representative of those who could not adjust: Unable to master Hebrew and find employment, they did not share Felicia's excitement about their new home country. After three years in Israel, Felicia's family emigrated once again, this time to Canada.

Felicia, in contrast to her parents, was able to adapt to new environments and cultures; she is a life-long learner with an innate taste for studying and expanding her horizons. Her thirst for education continued from Romania through to Israel and Canada. A graduate of the University of Bucharest, with an MA degree in Social Work from McGill University, Felicia's extraordinary talents and ambition are aptly demonstrated by the fact that, at age fifty, she started a PhD in counselling psychology.

This memoir brilliantly shows that people who choose to emigrate frequently have to deploy a particular type of tenaciousness: to be ready to start everything anew, to partition off one's previous educational or social background, and work their way up from entry-level positions and society's lowest-paying jobs. For their entire lives, immigrants frequently feel pulled between their two competing worlds of old and new. While this may cause internal frictions, it can also increase cultural sensitivity and empathy to others in need. Felicia herself shows shining versatility between the societies she experienced in the West and East, between religious and non-religious groups, between immigrant and local communities. As so many other Canadians who come from afar, Felicia is gifted with special sensibilities, and people like her undoubtedly make Canadian society a better place.

Across the Rivers of Memory is distinguished by its candour and a touching innocence. These characteristics make the story profoundly human, while opening up areas that are usually well guarded from public view. Felicia is candid, for example, about her rocky relationship with her mother, dysfunctions of her first marriage and the complicated relationship she has with her only daughter. With uncommon courage, she is also quick to laugh at herself. Felicia tells stories with a charming sincerity, filled with people who share faults and virtues side by side; the book's personalities are not "polished" in any moralizing way. Because of this bold frankness, we can contemplate the multiple facets of a Holocaust survivor's life. Memoirs like hers tremendously improve our understanding of survivors' wartime experiences and the repercussions that follow. This book will force the reader to think about a multitude of subjects. Among them will certainly be the meanings of identity, family, life, death and memory.

Diana Dumitru
Ion Creangă State Pedagogical University, Chisinau
2015

Acknowledgements

I would like to thank the Azrieli Foundation of Toronto for encouraging me to write this memoir. I would especially like to thank Linda Rosenbaum, volunteer interviewer for the Sustaining Memories program – a partnership between the Azrieli Foundation and Ryerson University – for transcribing our interviews and helping me put them in a linear sequence for clarity. I would also like to acknowledge editors Farla Klaiman, Arielle Berger and Andrea Knight, former managing editor, for their work on the memoirs, and I am very grateful to my good friend Karen Fainman for editing the expanded version of the original memoir, as well as for her constant support and encouragement along the way.

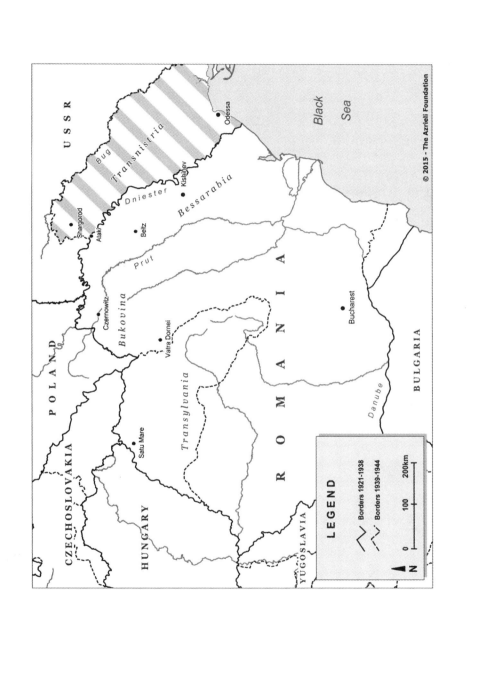

USSR

Odessa

Black Sea

Bug

Transnistria

Kishinev

Dniester

Bessarabia

Shargorod

Ataki

Beltz

Prut

Czernowitz

Bukovina

Vatra Dornei

Bucharest

R O M A N I A

POLAND

Transylvania

Danube

BULGARIA

Satu Mare

CZECHOSLOVAKIA

HUNGARY

YUGOSLAVIA

LEGEND

Borders 1921-1938

Borders 1939-1944

0   100   200km

N

Felicia Carmelly's Family Tree*

MATERNAL GREAT-GRANDPARENTS:
David Rubinger m. *Libba Druckman*

GREAT UNCLE:
Hersh

GREAT AUNT:
Charna

MOTHER:
Laura (Lipzia) m. ———

GRANDMOTHER:
Rivka (Rebecca) m. *Moses (Moshe) Siegler* ——— AUNT:
Sidi m. *Strulik Vollokh*

GREAT AUNT:
Anna

AUNT:
Mila m. *Armin Treiser* ———

GREAT UNCLE:
Alter

GREAT UNCLE:
Moishe

Elkhanan Steigman m. *Beile Rubinger*

AUNT:
Rachel

AUNT:
Etty m. *Molly Shufer*

SONS:
Ya'akov
Yuval

FATHER:
Isaac (Itzie) Steigman

*Felicia (Fella) Steigman (Carmelly)
born 1931
m. *Marcel*
remarried *Bill*

SONS:
Martin Brien
Erik Marcel
William Arthur

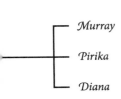

Murray
Pirika
Diana

DAUGHTER:
Ramona (Romy) m. *Richard*

To my daughter, Ramona (Romy) Joy Carmelly, and to all of my family members mentioned in this book, as well as their children and grandchildren.

Foreword

When Felicia first asked me to write something about my experience in editing the initial version of her memoir, I was taken aback. My intention was never to come forward with my voice, and I felt so strongly about this that I even shied away from Felicia's suggestion that she mention me in her acknowledgements. Yet, I was so touched by her insistence that I couldn't help but feel honoured by her request. I realized that she was trying to pass something on to me by asking me to do this, as if she were passing me the torch or asking me to step out onto the bimah as when turning bar or bat mitzvah.[1]

The experience of editing Felicia's book has been similar to my experience when I turned bat mitzvah – not chronologically speaking, at the age of twelve, but spiritually, through ritual, at the age of fifty. It was unusual for a woman from my generation to learn *maftir*, the concluding portion of the Torah reading on the Sabbath, as it wasn't the custom for a girl to have a bat mitzvah when I grew up. I had been raised not only as a secular Jew, but in a Jewish home where religion was frowned upon and considered a regression back to the more su-

---

1 For information on bar/bat mitzvah, as well as on other historical, religious and cultural terms; significant historical events and people; geographical locations; major organizations; and foreign-language words and expressions contained in the text, please see the glossary.

perstitious shtetl of the past rather than a move forward to the more progressive, modern era in which I had been born and raised.

But in facing my fiftieth birthday, on my own terms, I found it imperative to mark this important passage of time with a ritual that would be meaningful to me, and I could find no better marker than this spiritual Jewish coming-of-age ritual ceremony.

In learning the *maftir* later in life, I was able to really reflect on what I was learning. As I was grappling with the biblical text, I came to realize that the daily back-and-forth ritual of reading a complex passage where each and every vowel has a different note and every word a different meaning made me internalize the text in a way that I wouldn't have if the text had been straightforward. As I internalized more and more of the text, so too did I ingest more and more of my Jewish identity and meaning.

Just prior to my bat mitzvah, I found myself at the Holocaust Centre of Toronto, volunteering to be a docent introducing Holocaust survivor speakers. From there, as a volunteer member of Holocaust Education Week, I joined the Christian-Jewish Dialogue of Toronto, where I had the privilege of meeting an incredible woman with a spark to her like no other person I had met before. This woman, Felicia Carmelly, later became my close friend and confidante. In organizing an event at one of the churches, I requested that Felicia be the keynote speaker, as I knew that she would be a perfect match for the event.

After this experience, Felicia and I continued to meet as friends. Felicia later mentioned that she was surprised that I would want to be friends with someone her age. Little did she realize that I found it equally surprising that she would want to be friends with someone like me, with so little life experience, comparatively speaking, to her own. Even though Felicia and I had only met prior to my fiftieth birthday, she quickly became an honoured guest at my bat mitzvah.

While editing the first draft of Felicia's book, I realized that I was having a similar experience as I had in learning Torah. As I became closer and closer to the text and to Felicia's story, I grappled with my own collective history and soul as a Jew.

I remember one of my rabbi's speeches in which he said that being Jewish wasn't something that you could teach but rather something that you had to find for yourself and that when you did, you would know it. He was right. For those of us who have searched for meaning as Jews, it is possible that our identity has always been part of who we are; we simply needed it to be uncovered and discovered.

Once I discovered my meaning, I thirsted for a collective Jewish memory. Having close to four thousand years of history to remember can be a daunting task. And with so many survivors now departing from us with stories still untold, those concerned about Jewish identity are scrambling to see that our history not be lost from our collective consciousness. But I am glad to find that I am not alone in this endeavour. If my small effort contributes to this massive collective history in any way, I am happy. For those who allow me to make this contribution, like Felicia, I am most grateful. I listen carefully to what Felicia tells me because of the deep respect I have for the lessons she has learned.

Remembering our past is more than reflecting back on one of the most traumatic parts of our history. Felicia's book is more than that. It is a reminder of what can happen when you have internalized the trauma of the past and transcended it. The collective history of the Jews is ultimately about Life, not Death. It is about our incredible resilience to live life, as Felicia might say, against all odds. Felicia's vibrancy of life as reflected in this book is testimony to that.

Felicia was once asked what she thought that the responsibility of this generation of post-Holocaust Jews is. As she said, we have the responsibility to remember. Once we remember, we need to embrace our life and, with the lessons learned from our collective memory, live it to the fullest.

The most important thing that I have learned through my experience of participating in editing this memoir is that remembering is worthwhile. Something unexpected and wonderful happens in the process of remembrance. When you devote a part of your life to re-membrance, each layer of your memory turns into a new stratum of the collective four-thousand-year-old foundation, a thin woven lay-er in the most beautiful fabric that one can behold, that of Jacob's multicoloured cloth.

Karen Fainman

Author's Preface

I was motivated to write this memoir to help fill in the gaps of my family history for my younger cousins and their children, who are presently scattered across several continents. As the lone survivor from the older generation of my family, I would like to share with them, while I am still able to do so, answers to the outstanding inquiries they might have posed to their parents.

Most of the information gathered here about our family is from the lineage of my maternal grandparents. I regret not being able to explain much about my paternal grandparents and their immediate family but, given that they lived in the same geographic area as my maternal family, I am guessing that both lived with similar threats and insecurities.

From the multiple experiences I have had during my life, I chose, in this memoir, to describe some that truly forged my character and my values. Some of the memories are humorous; others portray serious challenges. Although I have written about my successes, I have specifically chosen to include some of my failures, which were caused by my own actions or by unfavourable circumstances. Despite the many years of pain failures may have brought me, most have enriched my life, teaching me many valuable lessons. Most importantly, more often than not, failure gave me the opportunity to start again.

Two underlying emotional states weave through my past: panic/anxiety and sadness/guilt. I believe my panic and anxiety derive from our Jewish history. Whereas many other people have had to struggle with poverty, diseases and disabilities, the Jewish people always had an additional sword hanging above their heads, that of antisemitism. Our ancestors were exposed to the virus of antisemitism for more than two thousand years. The bloody paths of their history were marked with pogroms, expulsions and persecutions. I think that in Jewish families, long before the world wars, panic and anxiety were rampant and were an understandable reaction to hatred by others. This angst was transmitted from one generation to the next for many centuries. And I no doubt inherited it.

There are two periods in my life about which I feel profoundly sad and guilty because they had terrible repercussions for my loved ones. One area that I wish I could do over again was raising my daughter, Ramona (Romy). By the time she was born in 1964, I was well marinated in the juices of anxiety and panic attacks and she, naturally, absorbed them from me. After many turbulent years in our relationship we both had the good sense to try to heal our pain. I love my daughter dearly and am deeply grateful to her for her willingness and commitment to open up and work through our pain together.

Another deep regret is my belief in and commitment to communism when I was still a teenager. My allegiance to this ideology prevented my parents from leaving Romania soon after the war, when they were younger. Had they been able to do so, I believe that they would have adapted more easily to their new environments and succeeded in them. My parents' suffering became more severe during the communist era, making it impossible for them to adapt to yet another culture, climate and lifestyle when we were finally permitted to emigrate from communist Romania. Unfortunately, my naïveté caused my parents much grief, and the depth of damage from their pain was impossible to undo.

After World War II, when we remaining survivors of the Holocaust reached countries that allowed us freedom, we were shocked by the reality of our losses: most of our family members had been murdered and our homes had been occupied by our enemies or, even worse, by our neighbours. Despite the emotional trauma this left us in, something incredible occurred: many of us had the courage not only to start all over again, but to avidly contribute to all the countries in which we settled.

The most important insight I have learned in my life is that ideas are more resilient and resistant than any parasite. Once the seed of an idea is implanted in the fertile ground of the brain, it is almost impossible to eradicate. It sticks in one's unconscious mind, making all conscious thoughts vulnerable. Because of the power of ideas, we must be vigilant in guarding our minds.

What we do *not* allow into our mind is just as important as, or perhaps even more important than, what we do allow. According to new age philosophy's Law of Attraction, the universe returns to us in greater volume the quality of the energy that our brain generates. The concept is that if a person does good, good will be returned to him sevenfold. Conversely, we need to be careful with negative thoughts, which attract negative energy. You can determine what kind of energy you will allow into your mind, which, in turn, will affect your health, well-being, relationships and contribution to the community you live in. And so, if you want love to come into your life, it is imperative that you use any means you can to get rid of hatred. One of the most profound biblical quotes is, "For as he thinketh in his heart, so is he" (Proverbs: 23:7).

People have told me that I come across as a full, vibrant force of nature. To the outside world this may be so. Yet, internally, I have been living for most of my life with panic and anxiety. Nonetheless, there have been many periods in my life during which I have experienced genuine happiness. I don't remember where I read the verse below, but I like it and want to share part of it.

Happiness keeps you sweet,
Trials keep you strong,
Sorrows keep you human,
Failures keep you humble,
Success keeps you glowing.

Anonymous

Generations

I gathered information about my family history from my relatives who had lived under the Soviet regime and, after its downfall in 1991, immigrated to Israel. According to them, our first known ancestor was my great-great-grandfather Avraham Rubinger from Poland. Avraham was a Torah scribe, an honoured role in the community, where religious exactitude was paramount. Avraham's job included meticulously writing scriptures – following religious law that tolerated no mistakes in transcription – and overseeing and training other scribes to do the same. His wife, whose name remains unknown, was a midwife. As was typical for women during that time, she was the breadwinner of the family, allowing her husband the necessary time to devote his life to the work of God. They lived in Poland, close to the border with Romania.

My great-great-grandfather and grandmother had six sons – the name of only one is known, David – and one daughter, Leah. I heard that the family was so poor that the boys had only one decent pair of pants and had to take turns wearing them to be able to go with their father to shul on Saturdays. As the boys grew up, they became herdsmen for a few cattle owners, aspiring to become cattle owners in their own right as a means of rising out of the poverty in which their father's generation had raised them. Believing that the pastures on the Romanian side had "greener" grass, the more ambitious elder brother persuaded the whole family to uproot from Poland and move to Romania, where, with the frugal savings they had managed to accumulate over the years, they purchased a little herd of their own.

Settled in a new country, the next generation, David and Libba (née Druckman) Rubinger took on roles similar to those of their parents: David became a Torah scribe and Libba a midwife, the breadwinner; both were still normative honourable roles in Jewish society. They had six children: Hersh, Charna, Rivka (Rebecca), Alter, Anna, and Moishe. Rebecca was my grandmother. My maternal and paternal grandmothers both come from the Rubinger family. They were first or second cousins.

Unlike the previous generation, which was destined for poverty, for the new generation wealth was now a possibility. Although wealth did not protect a Jew from bigotry, it did allow for a sense of confidence in confronting it. Eventually, one of the boys, Moishe, became a lawyer and a philanthropist. One story goes that once, sporting a nicely trimmed beard and dressed in a black suit and a vest with a pocket, out of which was hanging the chain of a watch, he was travelling by train to see a client. Across from him sat a farmer, who after a while smiled and said to him, "Hey, Jew, what time is it?" Without blinking an eye, Moishe smiled back and said, "If you can see through my pants that I am a Jew, you can also see what time it is."

My grandmother Rebecca married Moses (Moishe) Siegler, and they lived in Dorna, Romania. They had three daughters – Laura (Lipzia), Sidi and Mila. Rebecca gave birth to her third daughter, Mila, while her husband was at war. When Moishe died in World War I fighting on what we now call the "wrong side," my grandmother became a war widow. Now, not only did she not have an income, but she also had three daughters who needed dowries. At that time there weren't pensions or other types of assistance for war widows but as a privilege, the government allowed them to sell cigarettes and tobacco from a little table set up in front of a regular store.

When I lived in Israel years later, I met people who knew my grandmother when she was young. They told me that she would get up at four in the morning to collect branches and firewood to bring to other war widows for heating their houses in the winter. They say she did this before she went to set up her tobacco table. I think this is such a Jewish characteristic – not that other people aren't considerate and compassionate – but the idea of *tikkun olam*, repairing the world, is so ingrained in Jews. I can't believe that my grandmother had the energy to help others while taking care of three girls and Phillip, an orphaned boy of a distant relative whom she took in, managing her household and also selling tobacco at her table. I called her Omama, and I loved her so much.

To my grandmother's chagrin, her youngest daughter, Mila, married Armin Treiser, whose family was unknown to her. He was originally from Transylvania, and a newcomer in town. The couple made their home in Dorna. Sidi married Strulik Vollokh, a tourist in Dorna who was a well-to-do man from Beltz, Bessarabia, and she moved there.

Laura, the eldest, was my mother. Before she got married to my father, my mother was in love with a different man, but my father-to-be was very much in love with her and was also better off financially than the man she loved. Therefore, my grandmother insisted she marry my father, who would hopefully help with the dowries for her two younger daughters. Since my mother had no dowry, my paternal grandparents were not at all receptive to her and naturally, my mother resented them, as well as her own mother, since she was in love with someone else. This mutual animosity continued for the rest of their lives, and this is why I know very little about my paternal grandparents.

My mother eventually grew to love my father, but I never saw a word or sign of expression of love between them. Perhaps that was typical of that time. As Golde sings to her husband, Tevye, in *Fiddler on the Roof*, "For twenty-five years I've lived with him. Fought with him, starved with him. Twenty-five years my bed is his; if that's not love what is?"

My paternal grandparents, Elkhanan and Beile Steigman, had three children. The eldest was Rachel, who also fell in love with someone not to my grandparents' liking, but she married him anyway. Unfortunately, she died young, from an infection she contracted from an abortion. There's a story in the family about a Roma girl telling Rachel on the day of her wedding that she would die "two years from [her] wedding day," and that's exactly when she died. The next in line was my father, Isaac (Itzie), who was born in 1904 and given the Hebrew name Yitzhak. Both he and his younger sister, Etty, married against their parents' wishes.

A story in the family about my paternal grandparents is that they were supposedly so frugal that they ate from the same egg at breakfast in order to save money to build a house. I don't know if it's true, but I do know that my grandfather built our house with two apartments on the ground floor and two apartments on the second floor so that they could live in one and their three children could each have an apartment of their own in the same house. However, this arrangement didn't work out the way my grandparents had hoped. Rachel died, my father lived with his "unacceptable" wife in one of the second-floor apartments, and Etty lived with her parents on the ground floor only until she married Molly Shufer, a newcomer to Dorna. Two apartments were rented out.

I am the only child of my parents, Laura and Isaac Steigman. I was born Felicia (Fella) Steigman on September 25, 1931, in Vatra Dornei (Dorna) in the province of Bukovina, Romania. In Bukovina, which was part of the Austro-Hungarian Empire, most people spoke German, so my mother tongue is Austrian German. In speaking this language, we came to identify subconsciously with the "superior" Austrian culture. As Austrian-German-speaking Jews, we had a proud snobbishness about our Germanic-Austrian traits. We came to believe that we were superior to the Romanian-Jewish people from other areas of the country.

My mother was a very pretty and cheerful young woman. She was also an obsessive housewife and a marvellous cook. She baked pastries, pies and delicious, magnificently decorated cakes with sugar-blown fruits that seemed out of a photo in a magazine. There were always delightful aromas from the kitchen, and on Friday nights, the dinner table was ornate with candles, flowers and a special dessert for Shabbat. There were so many trays of delicious foods that I could hardly see our guests on the other side of the table! For a party, my mother made several cakes and tortes. I don't know how she did all of this; I'm a good cook, but I can't bake like she did. It's too precise for me.

We were what I call "modern-style kosher." My mother kept all the butter, dairy and meat in our icebox, and the iceman regularly brought long bars of ice on a hook to drop in the box. On Friday nights we ate fish, usually carp, which, when live, was stored in our bathing tub. In the fall, Mama took out the big copper cauldrons from the cellar and prepared all kinds of food for the winter – jars of fruit jams, honey butter and goose and chicken fat and livers. She covered the glass jars with special paper and put them in straight rows, like soldiers, on the wooden shelves in the cellar.

My mother was obsessive about feeding me all the time, which I obsessively resisted. I think Jewish mothers of the time wanted their children to have reserves of fat, "in case something bad happened." This was a particularly difficult situation for me because I was a poor eater to begin with. I'd walk around with food stored in my cheek because I didn't want to swallow it. At night, my mother would come to my bed and dig the food out from my cheek so I wouldn't sleep with it in there.

The only food I remember really liking was the skin of roasted chicken. When we had roasted chicken and chicken soup with noodles for dinner, I always took the skin from my piece of chicken and put it on the side of my plate to save it for the end. But my father, concerned that my mother would slap me because I hadn't finished eating the food, would take the skin off my plate and eat it when my mother wasn't looking. I used to think this was my father's and my little secret, but now I think that Mama just pretended not to see.

We were a middle-class family, living in a beautiful resort town nestled in the majestic northern Carpathian Mountains. During the summer months our little town spilled over with tourists from all over Romania and from other European countries who were seeking out our health spas, fresh mountain air and famous mineral waters. Even in the winter, our little town was filled with tourists. Spectators and participants alike came from far and wide for our ski competitions and other winter sports.

In the centre of town stood a large, beautifully landscaped park, which gradually receded into the forested peaks. Thousands of squirrels scampered throughout the park, so tame that they would boldly approach any passerby who might stretch out his or her hand with a peace offering of nuts. The heart of the park was the Casino, which had gambling, entertainment and glamorous, elegant balls. We used to watch the bejewelled ladies dressed in fancy silk, lace and velvet gowns, with hats decorated with feathers, fruit and flowers. They entered the Casino escorted by men dressed in tuxedos. This gave us a glimpse of just how fine the upper-class life could be. During World War II, the Casino was mostly visited by uniformed military men and card sharks.

The Jews lived primarily in the centre of town. In 1930, there were about 1,700 Jews in Dorna, out of a total population of 7,750. The Jewish population was mostly comprised of middle- and low-income earners, whose diverse occupations – merchants and shoemakers, teachers and tailors, doctors, dentists, barbers and bakers – contributed to the rich fabric of life. Some gentiles lived among us, while others lived farther out on farms and toiled the land. We lived very comfortably side-by-side with the non-Jewish population, on the most amicable of terms. We never hesitated to invite our neighbours to any family events or holidays.

It was not that antisemitism did not exist in Romania, it was just that it would come and go with such frequency and familiarity that Jews learned how to cope with it. Sometimes antisemitism reared its head and at other times it was underground. Inevitably, its ugliness would surface during some fabricated pretext that blamed Jews for one thing or another. Jews were familiar with this pattern, as it had gone on for many centuries, and we expected it to continue.

An Only Child

We had a peaceful, pleasant life, with a routine that gave us the security of more or less knowing what the next day would be like. The stores in Dorna, as in all of Europe, closed for lunchtime. My father had a haberdashery store where he sold all kinds of things, like needles, thread, fabrics, boots, fur muffs, fur hats and some clothing. His parents had a similar store on the same street. My father came home from his store for lunch, which was the main meal of the day, and a little siesta. Then he returned to the store until 6:00 p.m. Evenings, we had a light supper and then visited family or friends, or went for walks in the park or to the movies.

Like other women, my mother organized her household chores, based on a psychological need for security and structure, by designating each chore for a certain day of the week. I like the idea of a different activity every day and I think it was very smart for women of that time.

Monday was laundry day, and the linens were washed on a washboard and hung out in the attic, the third floor, to dry. My mother and the maid, Saveta, made everything sparkling white. Tuesday was for ironing clothes and cleaning shoes. Saveta ironed while my parents and I took our shoes out on the balcony to get the mud off, clean and polish them, and shine them up. The three of us worked together like on a conveyer belt, while we sang or joked. In addition, since we had a sewing machine at home, a dressmaker would come in whenever we needed to make repairs or to make us dresses. Wednesday was the grand cleaning day. Saveta and my mother cleaned and shined the crystal, silver and chandeliers and took the carpets out onto the balcony to be beaten. Thursday was market day in town. Farmers came in from the countryside, bringing their produce, eggs, butter and cheeses to sell to the city people. Then they went to the stores to buy clothes, shoes, fabrics and other goods. They also took this opportunity to visit doctors, dentists, shoemakers, tailors and the like. Since that was the busiest day of the week in the store, my mother went in to help out. On Thursdays, my mother also went to the market to buy food for the week. The milkman came to the house that day to bring us fresh milk, butter, eggs, cheese and sour cream.

The entire week centred on Shabbat, and Friday was spent cooking for Shabbat. Mother would make cookies, challah and cake. Someone came to the house in the morning to kill and clean the carp in the tub. Later in the day, we'd go to the steam bath, which we called the shvitz. I wasn't crazy about having to bathe naked with other women at the shvitz, but that's what all the families did. The baths were not too far from our synagogue, and we went there afterward. There were two synagogues in the city. One was strictly Orthodox and the other, which we went to, was "modern Orthodox." After we had prayed, we came home and ate Erev Shabbat (Sabbath evening) dinner. We lit candles after sundown, which may not have been right according to Jewish tradition, but that's what we did. On Saturday mornings my father and I went to shul, an occasion for which I would get to wear my nicest clothes. My mother did not come with us very often because she was busy preparing lunch, the main meal of the day. Sundays we often visited friends, went to a movie or had a party at our home for some occasion.

In our beautiful resort town, whether it was spring, summer or fall, we spent the afternoons going to the park, sitting on benches and listening to military bands playing in the gazebo. Peasant girls sold delicious wild strawberries, blueberries and raspberries they had just plucked from the forest. I brought nuts from home to feed the tame squirrels from my hand. Sadly, when the fascist Legionnaires were later in power, they poisoned thousands of squirrels in the park. I used to think that they killed them because they thought they were Jewish.

Life was easygoing and we had everything we needed. Our house had running water, which very few houses at the time had, and we even had a radio, which was also a rarity. The apartments in our house were built so each had a kitchen, dining-living room and bedroom. Each room had two doors, one leading from one room to the next and one leading out to a long balcony that spanned the length of each apartment. This was particularly convenient because when we rented one room to tourists, they could have their own exit to the outdoors.

I slept in the living room on a bed with a frilly lace bed cover and a beautiful reading lamp beside it, but I didn't like girly things when I was a child. I was more of a tomboy and liked jumping over fences or climbing up to rooftops. Though I never played with dolls, I did like playing dress-up with my girlfriends. We would go into our attic where old clothes, shoes and hats were stored in trunks and closets, take some of them out, and imagine ourselves as someone else. We usually played that we were some big shot's wife. One of us would pretend to be the wife of the King; one the wife of prime minister Marshal Antonescu (she had to be really mean); and another the wife of God (she had to be really, really good). But the most important one would dress up as Hitler's wife, who of course could do anything she wanted. It's interesting to me how, at such a young age, we understood, or misunderstood, the hierarchy of power. And whoever heard of God having a wife?

My play area was a little house in the yard. This was also our sukkah, a small building with a roof that could be opened during nice weather or for the holiday of Sukkot, the Festival of Booths. One time I organized a "factory" there and had all my friends cut out papers and sand dowels to manufacture pinwheels that turned and twirled when we ran with them. A group of kids came to the yard every day to make these things to sell to stores or to give to poor kids or to people at shul. It was our work, our production.

In 1940, when I was about nine years old, I remember having a funeral for a dead bird I had found in the backyard. I put it in a shoebox that I decorated all fancy with ribbons and shiny material, including something red to keep the "evil eye" away. I said a prayer for the bird and then marched through the city carrying the "coffin" with a convoy of kids behind me. Unfortunately, we were stopped by the cruel green-shirted Legionnaires, members of the fascist Iron Guard that had gained power that September. They told us that we couldn't walk in certain areas. This was my first encounter with the authorities, who were becoming increasingly antisemitic.

That fall, when I was supposed to be in Grade 3, I was expelled from school, but not for misbehaviour, and I was not alone. With growing antisemitism in Romania, all Jewish kids were kicked out of school. In my case, I was called in front of the class by the teacher, who pulled out her big black student attendance book and whacked me over the head with it, saying, "You can't come to school any more or ever again, and you'll never grow any taller because you're a Jew." Later, right before we were deported, she made a point of walking right by our house to gloat.

German troops started moving into Romania in October 1940. Through that winter and into 1941, a series of restrictions were implemented, and with them came a corresponding escalation of harassment of Jews. The entire atmosphere in town underwent a drastic transformation. Gone were our lovely family parties, spontaneous singing and relaxed strolling in the park. Curfews became mandatory and anyone caught on the street in the evening could be arrested and shot, without even undergoing a trial.

In our attic or cellar, our family and friends began secretly listening to foreign radio stations, like the BBC, hoping that someone, somewhere, would intervene. Everybody I knew seemed to be whispering all of the time. I was scared, but no one would talk to me about anything. I didn't quite understand why our life had changed so much, and I felt a deep fear growing in my belly. The adults were nervous and irritable. They appeared to be hiding something terrible. A physical distance slowly crept into our relationships with gentile friends, with whom we had been on such good terms. We realized that we were no longer welcome in their homes.

By August 1941, when we walked out of the house, we had to identify ourselves by pinning a yellow Star of David to our garments. Newer antisemitic rules continued to bombard us daily from the Romanian fascist government. Every morning at 10:00 a.m., a youngster from the Iron Guard beat his drum on the steps in front of City Hall and informed us about the new day's restrictions: the compulsory yellow star; changes in curfews, which were constant; prohibition on intermarriage; prohibition on selling alcohol (which meant that if you were a Jewish restaurant owner your business was pretty much finished, since a meal without wine was unheard of in Romania); no gatherings in synagogues; and no meetings, for that matter, of any kind. With each new restriction or prohibition, we felt more squashed and fearful.

I distinctly remember my tenth birthday in September 1941. For a child my age who had been given gifts on every possible occasion – as the only child in my immediate family, my uncles, aunts and maternal grandmother had always pampered me and showered me with gifts – I naively believed that this birthday would be no different. But things had changed so drastically that I did not receive one single present. There was no birthday party, no celebration. It felt like my family had forgotten me. Instead, when my parents came down from the attic, as was now their usual daily habit, as soon as they saw me they turned to each other with fingers on their lips in a shushing motion, so I would not hear what they were talking about. The more they shushed, the more afraid I became because I didn't know what they were shushing about. The "shhh" sound became a symbol of the continuous atmosphere of danger in my ten-year-old mind.

When I later asked my parents about this period in time, they admitted that they, along with most of the Jews in Romania, knew about the atrocities that were already then being perpetrated against the Jews in Poland, but truly, no one believed anything would happen to us. The Jews of Romania were no different from the Hungarian, French, Czechoslovak or other European Jews. Everyone was in denial and said the same thing. "Even if what is happening all around us is horrific, the Romanians [substitute Hungarians, French, Czechs, other Europeans] are such good people, they could not possibly do anything bad to us." This was the attitude among most European Jews. I later learned that some Jews did talk about leaving, while others tried to escape through the Black Sea on derelict ships heading to Palestine; some of these ships sank with their cargo of refugees, and others managed to reach our ancient homeland of Palestine.

Since we could not predict the day when the Romanians would take further action against the Jews, my mother tried to bring some sense of normalcy to our situation. After I was expelled from school, my mother and I took Hebrew and Jewish history lessons from a Jewish teacher who came to the house. He also taught me general subjects. I think Mama was preparing for us to flee to Palestine if things got worse.

In September 1941, one of the Romanian gendarmes, a formerly friendly neighbour, came into my father's store and warned him, "Take your family and leave now. You are in big danger." My father laughed in his face. Granted, the guy was half-drunk and had a beer bottle in his hand. But he was earnest about what he was trying to say and got so angry that my father did not take him seriously that he smashed my father in the face with the beer bottle. The bottle broke, and my father came home with his lip cut open, a broken nose and his face all black and blue. That man had wanted to save us, but we didn't realize it at the time.

Then things got really bad. The gendarmes rounded up all the men, including my father and uncle, and locked them into the bigger shul (synagogue) in town. Then the gendarmes drove around in trucks with loudspeakers, announcing that we, the Jewish community, must bring a huge amount of money and jewellery to City Hall or else the synagogue would be set on fire and the men burned alive.

After two days, my mother became incredibly anxious. In the late afternoon, we went to the shul. I looked through the window with her. I saw men lying on the floor and wondered whether they were sleeping or if they had fainted from the lack of food and water. The men looked awful, unwashed and unshaved.

By the time we started on our way back home, it was already dark, so my mother pulled out a flashlight from her handbag and pointed it downward so we wouldn't trip on the cobblestones. One of the gendarmes caught us and started swearing at us, yelling that we were dirty Jewish spies. He was convinced that we were using our flashlight to signal to whatever enemy airplanes he imagined were overhead, and he threatened to take us to the police station. My mother immediately emptied the contents of her purse into his pockets; the bounty seemed to appease him and he let us go home. The experience was so scary that when we got home that night, Mama didn't even make us supper. I cannot remember another day in my life when she had forgotten to feed me.

The men were held hostage in the synagogue for a few more days because not as much money or jewellery had been collected for ransom as the authorities had hoped. Then, something unexpected happened. The people in Dorna began to notice that there weren't any tradesmen or professionals to run things in the manner to which they had been accustomed and they were beginning to feel the impact. Without the Jewish men, there were hardly any bakers, shoemakers, dentists, doctors, lawyers and barbers. So the authorities slowly began letting the men out, one by one. The first group to be released was the bakers, so my clever uncle Armin said he was a baker and was let out. He did not know a thing about baking bread....

The moment my father was released, he came home and boarded up the corners of the attic by building false walls. He was creating storage space to hide basic dry goods and his purchases from town like soap, toothpaste, rice, sugar, needles, fabrics, boots and things that my mother decided were "strictly necessary."

Soon after this, a young Romanian officer and his wife came to our house to tell us that we would soon be deported and they offered to adopt me. They had not been able to have children of their own. My parents said they needed one day to think about it. That whole night, they sat in the kitchen and talked it over. Eventually they decided, "Where we go, she goes." Their answer was definitive.

When I grew up and could reflect on this with the mind of an adult, I felt so very grateful to my parents for making this difficult decision the way they did. Although they exposed me to a terrible risk, I cannot imagine how totally different my life would have been had they given me up. Besides losing my family, I would not have been raised as a Jew, which is core to my very being. My love for our history and our culture enriches my life. Also, I would not have gained the strength and fortitude I have today had it not been for my experiences during the war, which strengthened my will to live.

The Nightmare

I remember the cold, rainy autumn day in October 1941 when the youngster at City Hall announced that all Jews must be at the train station at 5:00 p.m. sharp. We were to pack food for three days and take only as much as we could carry. The youngster yelled out the order with a voice full of hatred, sneering at us with the authority of someone assigned full control over our destinies. Privately, to protect me from hearing, my father told my mother the final words of the ordinance. She repeated his words in shock: "Anybody found after the train has left will be shot."

Because we had been told to pack enough food for just three days, we naturally assumed, as any level-headed person might, that we would be returning home after three days. How could it possibly be otherwise? Such a thought was beyond our imagination. After packing, Mama started obsessively cleaning the house, demanding that I help her as she quickly moved from sofa to chair. I couldn't understand why. The house was already so clean; hadn't she cleaned it just the day before? I knew better than to question her – she was in such a terrible mood. We were ready to leave when Mama noticed that I had left my apron on the kitchen chair instead of hanging it up on the hook where it belonged. She screamed at me and I had to go and put it back in its place. That is how I remember the very last moment in our home.

My mother layered me in three pairs of long underwear, three sweaters and two coats, explaining as she was dressing me that it was very, very cold. It reminded me of my mother's compulsion to fatten me up with "reserves," always protecting me in case of an emergency. I was wearing my backpack when we left to walk to the train station. My parents carried the heavy bundles as well as pots full of food: schnitzels, which my mother had made that day from chicken breasts, and hearts of wheat as a side dish. We had just enough for three days for the three of us.

At the station, I stood with my parents, surrounded by our family: my aunt Mila and uncle Armin Treiser; my maternal grandmother, Rebecca Siegler; and my paternal grandparents, Beile and Elkhanan Steigman. A little farther away were more aunts, uncles and cousins. Most of the adults around us were silent, as if hypnotized; some were moaning and groaning. Kids were chattering and babies were crying. Now and then there was a burst of screaming when someone lost their child or their parents in the crowd. I asked myself, "How come everybody is travelling tonight, all at the same time, all to the same place, all with the same train?"

I saw that passenger trains were coming and leaving without stopping for us and knew instinctively that something was off. It was almost dark, getting colder, and we were still waiting in the rain. We began to get impatient. "In the train, it will be warm," I reassured myself. I was leaning against my mama and closed my eyes. We stood there from about 5:00 p.m. until 9:00 p.m., with passenger trains going back and forth, back and forth. To keep my mind busy, I was thinking about how cold it was in the forest and how the animals must be freezing. I felt bad for them.

Suddenly, a very long, brown train pulled in and stopped. It was a cattle train meant for beasts, not people. The doors, as big as walls, slid open with a thud. The soldiers were screaming at us, shouting, swearing, pushing, pulling, and barking orders for us to get in. Frantically, people began running, slipping in the mud, falling down and getting up. Everybody was moving and yelling. We were being herded with rifle butts into the cars. For a few minutes, I couldn't see my parents. I panicked. Then, I fell in the mud and got a nosebleed. Somebody stepped on my hand. "Don't step on me!" I yelled. I was pulled from the mud. I was afraid Mama would be angry because there was mud and blood all over my face, my mittens and my coat. The next thing I knew, I was picked up and thrown into the train.

After hours of waiting in the cold rain, we were stuffed, body touching body, into the train and the huge doors were slammed shut. The train stood in the station for at least two more hours before surging violently forward. We had no idea to where, for how long or why we were being taken away from our homes.

The floor of the cattle car was covered with fresh, wet manure. The stench was oppressive, horrible. I later understood the manure was intentional, part and parcel of the dehumanization process. You know what was on my ten-year-old mind at that moment? Where I would go to the bathroom. The thought of voiding in public horrified me. I asked my mother and she said, "Well, here, go!" "In my underwear? Standing up?" "Yes," she said. This answer came from an obsessively clean woman who used to be angry when I came home from school with the slightest hint of mud on my shoes. Her "Go" was painful, awful. We were all standing with our own shit and pee inside our clothes and surrounded by manure, like beasts in the cattle car, as the fascists intended.

I think I suffered more than the adults in the train because breathing was barely possible for someone as small as me, squeezed into the adults surrounding me. To keep my mind distracted, I conjured up a game with myself. Because we were all so squished, I thought, let me see how far I can lean without falling.

At the beginning of the train ride, there was a fight in the cattle car; desperate for air, everybody wanted to sit near the small air vent. It soon turned out to be one of the worst places to be. Since there was no pail for the call of nature, after eating, people used empty pots for that purpose. The men broke metal bars on the vents so the pots could be emptied out through the vent. It was soon discovered that, when dumped through the vent of a moving vehicle, the urine and feces came right back into their faces. When this first happened, the people who had the bad fortune of sitting there began screaming hysterically. While they screamed, others sang, cried or prayed. My mother summarized this period as the time when some people "went out of their minds," but I didn't know what that meant then.

I remember a woman in our car holding her screaming baby to her breast. Some people were yelling at her to quieten the baby, but she couldn't, I think because her breast milk had stopped due to her high level of stress. As the baby continued to scream, the tension continued to escalate. In desperation, she unpinned a brooch from her lapel, pricked her nipple until the blood squirted out and quickly pushed it into the baby's mouth. The baby stopped crying for a few minutes. But then it started again.

We suffered on this cattle train for three full days and three full nights. The train did stop from time to time, though not for our benefit, of course – only to remove the dead. Before the dead were unloaded, I had been certain that these people were sleeping. Only a kid, I had never seen a dead person before. The train stopped at each and every major city en route to retrieve all hospitalized, mentally ill Jews, who were also under deportation orders.

After three gruelling days, we reached a little town on the shore of the River Dniester called Ataki. We were told that we would remain there for a few days. Had we travelled directly to this destination, it should have taken only a half day, as it was not too far from Dorna.

Once a thriving Jewish town, Ataki was bombed out and in total ruins. Not a single resident who had lived there before the war could be found. The soldiers let us out of the train and ordered us to go out and seek shelter wherever we could find it. In one of the houses we found two rooms where the ceilings were relatively intact to shelter us from the freezing rain and snow.

The next day, my mother decided to take me to the river to clean up after our hellish three days' journey. In her mind, it was a bigger risk to go on so filthy than to be caught by the soldiers guarding us. I was looking forward to feeling clean once again. We went to the river very early in the morning, hoping the soldiers would still be asleep. It was barely light outside. When we got to the water, we were horrified by the gruesome sight that we encountered: dead bodies and limbs of people and horses, and torn up, bloodied Jewish prayer books and Torah scrolls were scattered all over the river bank. Mother somehow mustered up the strength to wash herself and me despite this.

On our way back to where the rest of the family was, the soldiers spotted us and started shooting. We both fell to the ground and began crawling, my mother on top of me so the bullets wouldn't hit me. We managed to stumble into a dark cave to hide. After our eyes adapted to the darkness, we saw some writing on the walls in Hebrew. Painted in blood on the stone walls, the writing said, "Please say Kaddish [the Jewish prayer for the dead] for the many people who were murdered here." My mother cried when she saw this. After a few hours, when we calculated the soldiers would be having lunch, we crawled back to the shelter. The rest of the family was relieved to see us.

After another night in Ataki, the Romanian soldiers herded us up a steep, slippery, muddy hill. They cursed and shouted at us and at each other because there was freezing rain and getting up the hill was quite difficult, even for them in their sturdy army boots. For us, walking up the hill would have been next to impossible had we not already rid ourselves of almost all of our possessions. We could not help but wonder if this walk was arranged precisely for that purpose, so the soldiers wouldn't have to demand our baggage from us.

When we reached the top of the hill we came to a large barn with a thatched roof supported by wooden posts. The floor was full of dry manure, on which we readily lay down to catch our breath. Almost immediately, people fell asleep from the sheer exhaustion of the train ride and the climb up the muddy, slippery hill. Compared to the stench of the fresh manure in the train, the dry manure on the floor was not as suffocating. Meanwhile, since we did not know what danger to expect next, the men organized themselves into pairs to stand on guard near the posts and observe what was happening outside. Gone forever was the security of life's predictability, the organization of structured activities each day of the week at home. Now, we lived from one minute to the next, in fear of what new calamities awaited us.

At midnight, we were woken by loud screaming. Startled, we ran to the openings to see what was happening. I pushed my head between the legs of a man and saw frightening creatures running and howling like wolves all around the barn. They had what appeared to be fluttering white capes on their shoulders and under the capes they were stark naked. After a few minutes their screaming was accompanied by gunshots, and in about half an hour all was dead silent again. We had no idea what was happening, but were glad that the shooting had stopped and had not penetrated the inside of the barn. As frightened as we were, most of us fell asleep again.

In the morning, we woke up to the sight of dead bodies lying in the mud. My father bribed a soldier by giving him his watch for an explanation of what had happened during the night. The soldier told him that after leaving us in the barn, the soldiers had walked down the hill, collecting all the bundles that we had discarded. They then went to the train and opened up the three last train cars and pulled out the mentally ill Jews who had been collected from the various hospitals. These people were naked, wrapped only in bedsheets from the hospitals, as they were not given clothes when the soldiers forcibly removed them.

The soldiers, just for laughs, had decided to organize a performance mimicking an ancient European myth that the dead rise from their graves at midnight. They had bound the nearly one hundred patients with a rope. No, not because they were afraid of any of them escaping, but because they wanted to make sure that the entire group got to the barn at the same time.

The soldiers herded them up the hill and exactly at midnight they let the terrified patients loose around the barn. Once the "prank" was over, the soldier told my father, "We yelled at them to stop running, but they did not obey our orders, so we used them as target practice." Stop running? These poor people had travelled without food, water or medication for between one and three days, depending on where they had been picked up. They were freezing, starving and scared to death. They had been awakened in the middle of the night, roped and herded up a hill. Anyone would have been hysterical in this situation, let alone the mentally ill. Anyone in their right mind would not have stopped running. The soldiers had succeeded in re-enacting the ancient European mythical performance: to me, they looked like dead people coming out of the grave.

A few days later, the soldiers took us down the hill again to the shore of the Dniester, where a huge barge was waiting for us, surrounded post to post by a thick rope. They herded us onto the barge, which went back and forth transporting more and more people across the river. Not everyone made it onto the barge. Dozens of Jews were herded directly into the river on foot and either drowned or were shot. On the barge, I hung on to the rope; my parents stood behind me. Right beside me stood the young woman and baby from the train. She was holding her baby in one arm and a bundle of rags used for diapers in the other. She looked tired and pale and stood like a statue, unable to move. Her baby was quiet this time. I could hear the roaring of the waves as I held the rope tightly. Suddenly, the young woman stretched out her arm and let the baby fall into the dark waves. I thought she had dropped the baby by mistake and would soon start to scream. You can't imagine how I felt when no one said a word. In retrospect, I think some people didn't react because the deportation and all that had followed made them feel dehumanized. My mother whispered to my father, "She dropped the baby deliberately to spare the child further suffering." My father said, "Maybe the baby was already dead."

When we arrived on the other side of the Dniester, the soldiers once again began screaming, swearing and shoving us. They searched everybody as they disembarked, demanding all of the contents of our pockets: money, fountain pens, watches, rings, earrings. My earrings were not noticed then. Later, when they were, a soldier tore them from my ears, making blood ran down my neck. I remember Mama silently wiping it off.

We had arrived at the shores of a big city called Mogilev, one of the four transit points into Transnistria. I learned later that the name Transnistria had been coined from two words, "trans" and "Nistria," meaning "across the River Dniester" to designate a 16,000-square-mile piece of land in southwestern Ukraine. The name Transnistria was not on any pre-war map – it existed only from the summer of 1941 to the spring of 1944.

Before World War II, the Dniester River was the border between Romania and the Ukrainian Soviet Socialist Republic. In 1941, when the German Nazis occupied the Ukraine, they put this territory under Romanian administration as a reward for Romania having joined the Axis Powers against the Allies. To the east and west, this piece of land was bordered by two big rivers, the Dniester and the Bug; all "settlements" in Transnistria, big or small, were designated as either ghettos or camps – transit, concentration, labour or death camps. There was not a single city, town, village or collective farm that was exempt. Transnistria served as a massive ghetto for Jews, with no possibility of escape. Geographically, Transnistria became the largest killing field in the Holocaust.

Death Surrounded Us

After a few days in Mogilev, where we stayed in a bombed-out factory, we were told to get ready for another long trip, this time on foot. This turned out to be a death march – the Romanian soldiers did everything they possibly could to cause the death of as many Jews as possible.

We were forced to march in the freezing cold through the countryside for three days, seeking shelter along the way among the Ukrainian Jews living in shanties in the villages. Some people gave us food, and we dug up frozen vegetables left behind by farmers. The soldiers did not seem to mind that we ate – I'm sure they were convinced that no one would survive this journey. In retrospect, I believe that the soldiers hoped most of us would die on these roads rather than find shelter.

The elderly and sick were left behind if they couldn't keep up with the soldiers' pace. My grandmother was having a difficult time, and I was so worried about her. We couldn't help her because whoever went to help someone in need would be shot. As a result, many of the young children, the elderly and the sick were left behind to die of starvation or be devoured by wild animals. The roads were lined with fresh cadavers bloated from hunger or partially ripped open by animals. These were the victims of previous convoys of deportees.

What stayed in my memory most from this horrible march was

the skull of a little girl with blonde curls. Nothing remained of her but bones and hair. This left such a terrible impression in my mind that even now I still dream of her.

I also recall a peasant passing by our group on a wagon. He stopped when he noticed a deportee in our line with a coat he liked. He told the soldier he would like to have it, and the soldier took his gun, shot the man and allowed the peasant to take the coat. How cheap a Jewish life was at that time.

Walking was incredibly difficult for us because the roads were muddy and full of holes. We marched on these muddy roads faster and faster, herded together, surrounded by well-dressed, well-fed and well-armed soldiers. We were hungry beyond belief, exhausted, frightened and deeply depressed. After the war, people asked me, "Why did you not fight the soldiers?" These people had no idea that even moving out of line by as much as three inches would mean a severe beating or shooting.

After three days of being dragged from one village to the next, we reached Shargorod, a ghetto, where we finally found shelter with a Jewish family. Some of the deportees had marched less and some longer to find shelter. People were constantly knocking on doors, asking to be taken in for the night. If they were lucky, they were allowed in. We were completely dependent on whether or not local Jews would take us in, either because we had something to give in exchange for shelter or if by chance they wanted to be charitable.

We managed to find shelter with a family of five. Simion, the head of the family, was an accountant on a collective farm situated about one hour away from the town. We never met him, as he had already been recruited into the Soviet Red Army. Beila, his wife, was a very attractive young woman. Her son from a previous marriage, ten-year-old Tosia, was a handsome, placid boy. Beila and Simion's five-year-old son, Musia, was a smart, conniving, freckled redhead. And Simion's mother, referred to simply as "Babushka," grandmother, was an old, extremely wrinkled woman. Even though the family lived in a shack with only one kitchen and two large rooms, they took in eighteen more people to live with them. I think that Babushka was initially open to this idea because she assumed that our stay was temporary and that we would depart in the next few days.

We had a difficult time speaking to our hosts because we didn't have a common language. They spoke Yiddish and Ukrainian, and we spoke German and Romanian. However, the similarities between Yiddish and German made some communication possible.

To accommodate all of the people in such a cramped little hut, the men located some old wooden boards from a dilapidated shack and built a makeshift second floor for sleeping. After a few days there, my mother became paralyzed from the waist down; perhaps this was a reaction to fear, but more likely it was due to her extreme aversion to the dirt we were living in. The fact that there was no running water was bad enough. But even worse was the transformation of the little postage stamp of a backyard into a giant latrine for twenty-two. There was a pond in the middle of the yard that soon became our public toilet. People would just sit around it, doing their business. Because this same water was also used for our washing and cooking, dysentery became rampant. This public toilet had a particularly traumatic effect on me. Since I was about to begin puberty, I was very shy about nudity and found relieving myself in public so embarrassing that to this day I cannot use a public toilet. After about six months in Shargorod, the paralysis in the lower part of my mother's body slowly lifted and she eventually started to move again. This was a true miracle.

Our shelter was very small, relative to how we had lived before. Even though there was barely any furniture in it, when we walked we couldn't help but bump into each other. In the hut there was a built-in iron oven that Babushka used for baking bread or cooking, if she had anything to cook. Friends from the collective farm where Simion had worked occasionally brought some potatoes, grains, cabbage, onions or beans. If she had enough to share, she did, but when her bounty was limited, she naturally kept it for her family.

Death surrounded us. Our men had to dig mass graves. We became accustomed to waking up to dead bodies in the shack. Sometimes we couldn't tell who was dead and who was alive. I witnessed people who were unable to get up because their hair had frozen to the floor. The hair had to be cut off to enable them to stand up. It was terrible.

It was not long before we all became infested with lice and bedbugs. Babushka laughed at us if we complained about the lice. "What are you so upset about? This is a sign that you are alive," she would say. What she meant, of course, is that when a person is alive the lice feed on his blood. But once someone has died, the lice march like a miniature army away from the dead body in search of the next live body to feed on. Little highways of lice led everywhere.

When we still had a few possessions, we exchanged them for food. The peasants brought some potatoes, beans, beets or corn flour in exchange for a clothing item such as a dress, blouse or pair of stockings. One woman gave us quite a few bags of vegetables for Mother's pink satin nightgown: the woman planned to use it as a wedding gown for her daughter. We also needed gasoline to wash my waist-long hair in order to kill the lice and the nits; unfortunately, besides killing the bugs, the gasoline also burned terribly when applied to the scalp. It was strange – even though we didn't actually use money for exchange, there was a clearly understood exchange rate: a pair of men's pants was worth a dozen eggs; shoes were worth two loaves of bread.

On rare occasions, we saw German soldiers in Shargorod, but they had nothing to do with the day-to-day conditions and slaughtering going on around us. It was the Romanian soldiers and Ukrainian police who guarded us and did the "dirty work." When the Romanian soldiers forced men to fix roads and bridges or dig mass graves, the men would get a piece of black bread from the army for their labour. The women and children started knitting socks, scarves and mittens for the peasants and for the army in exchange for some vegetables or oil. Unfortunately, the peasants brought us rough, homespun wool and instead of knitting needles, which they didn't have, they brought rough metal wires. After ten minutes of knitting, our fingers bled and everything we knitted turned red.

There was no heating other than the stove where Babushka occasionally cooked and baked. It remained warm from the daytime fire when there was something to cook, and she slept on top of it at night to keep warm. Inside the shack, there were so many of us huddled together all of the time that I don't remember being cold, although maybe that was because I slept on the top platform that the men had built. The people who slept under the platform on the floor were quite cold.

From time to time, Babushka was given a bottle of homemade vodka by friends from the collective farm. She hid it on the top shelf of a homemade wooden cabinet. When she wasn't looking, her grandson, Musia, climbed up on a wooden stump and took a few sips from the bottle. Discovering that her grandson had drunk vodka, Babushka would curse him, saying things like "You should get blisters on your tongue" and "You should grow with your head in the ground like an onion." Much later in my life, I heard that Musia became an alcoholic. How true this is, I do not know.

~

For the Jewish people, learning is extremely important. And so, even in the ghetto, parents sought out ways to ensure that their children went to "school." My parents learned that five shanties down the street from us lived a woman named Mme Victor who used to be a teacher. For a while, I went with four girls from different families and different towns in Romania to Mme Victor's shanty and sat on her dirt floor three times a week as she taught us about geography and history. There were no books, no pencils and no paper. We were "the People of the Book" without any books.

To forget about this miserable life, I often imagined that I was back home in my room, with my frilly bedcover, playing with toys or getting dressed up to go somewhere. Years later, I heard from survivors whom I interviewed for Steven Spielberg's Survivors of the Shoah Visual History Foundation that they also daydreamed about life before deportation, just as I did.

During this time I had a crush on the ten-year-old boy, Tosia; he always had his eyes on me. When my family could no longer exchange anything for gasoline and my mother had to cut off my hair, I was afraid that Tosia would no longer find me attractive. And when my fingers bled from knitting the rough wool, I was equally as preoccupied with how Tosia might react. It was the first time that I had ever flirted with a boy. It was so odd how attracted we were to each other given that we couldn't speak to one another. In my eyes, Tosia was so handsome that no later date could compare with him.

In the spring, summer and fall, we were allowed to go to the edge of the fields and do field work in exchange for red beets, potatoes, or a jug of oil, which was most important for cooking. We always shared what we had among ourselves. We were never guarded when we worked in the fields. It was unnecessary – if you ran away from one ghetto or camp and were lucky enough not to be devoured by wild animals, you would only end up at another. Even the ghettos and camps that were close to either of the two large rivers, the Dniester and the Bug, offered no opportunity for escape, because it was impossible to swim across them.

~

My paternal grandparents, Elkhanan and Beila Steigman, had been deported with us, as had Uncle Armin and Aunt Mila, but they all lived in other shacks in Shargorod. I'm not sure how it had been decided for us to live separately from my paternal grandparents, but it was the right arrangement because the relationship between them and my mother was not the best. They both passed away in the winter of 1941-42. I don't know how they died. One night shortly after they died, when my father was working at loading the mass grave, he looked for their bodies but did not find them. When he returned in the morning, he had a completely white patch of hair on the back of his head that had not been there before. How the stress affected his body in that manner is an enigma for me. I've never heard of such a thing, but I saw it with my own eyes.

As I mentioned, the deportees had to dig mass graves manually. In the winter, this couldn't be done because the ground was frozen, so a scrawny horse with a broken carriage came by once or twice a day to collect the dead bodies. Usually these were put out in front of the shacks and then thrown onto the carriage. The bodies were transported and piled up at the wall of a derelict synagogue in town. This mound was soon huge. In the spring, when the thaw started, animals would start pulling on the bodies and people became extremely upset, so the men were ordered to hack the frozen bodies into pieces so they could fit in the graves left open from the fall.

One day, Babushka got some firewood from the collective farm and since all the adults were sick with typhoid fever and some were delirious, I was going to chop some wood in front of the hut. I was very cold, I had no gloves, and the rusty axe was terribly heavy. On the very first chop I cut myself and started to cry as I watched the blood colouring the white snow. Suddenly, I felt somebody behind me and turned around. I saw an officer in Romanian uniform standing about ten feet away from me. He was smiling and very slowly came closer. I thought, This is the end for me. I had nowhere to run. When he took the axe and raised it, I was sure that he was going to chop me to pieces, but he started chopping the wood and then helped me take it in to the shanty, where he talked with some of those who were less delirious. He told us that his name was Peter, his wife was Jewish and they had a cute three-year-old boy. With tears in his eyes, he said that he had no idea where his family was. He only knew that after he was mobilized to the army, they had been deported to a concentration camp. For the next two weeks Peter came to us almost every day and brought us medicine and some food. Then he disappeared and we never found out if his army unit moved or if, God forbid, somebody found out about him helping us and he was punished; for all we knew he could have been shot. I will never forget Peter, and I will always be very grateful to him.

Throughout our time in Shargorod, people got sick and died from many things – malnutrition, dysentery, starvation, freezing, typhus, typhoid fever, sheer exhaustion or shooting sprees, which occurred especially on Sundays, Christmas and New Year's Day, in various districts in Transnistria. Thousands of people were murdered. The bodies were just pushed into ravines, rivers or mass graves.

Some Jews managed to bribe the authorities and dig personal graves rather than have their loved ones interred in a mass grave. I know some Israeli survivors who went back in 1999 to what used to be called Transnistria to search for individual graves and say Kaddish, yet they found no sign of the graves. They appealed to elderly locals to find any remnants, and I heard that they found some bones in the soil. One survivor I know brought a tombstone and tools with him, as well as a metal railing to protect the grave he restored. When he came back the next day to say Kaddish, he found the stone and railing stolen, the gravesite demolished. I know another person who went back to Transnistria in the year 2000 to find a mass grave. When he could not locate it, he bribed a policeman to go with him to the forested area. He brushed away the autumn leaves with his boots, only to uncover cement, which had been poured over the grave. Another one found bones sticking out from the eroded soil.

I think we were all robotic while in Transnistria. We had been thrown from a lovely lifestyle into horrible squalor and an ever-present threat to our lives. Yet, in the midst of our tragedy, some babies were born and some even survived. Near our shanty lived a young married couple who had just had a baby. The woman was worried that her husband would be taken either to dig mass graves or to do forced labour at the Bug River, where she feared that he would be killed. Not wanting him to go, his wife took a pot of boiling water and threw it on his legs so they wouldn't take him. He remained in the shanty, but was forever crippled.

Years later, when I asked a woman who gave birth to her son in Transnistria when he was born, she answered, "On Pesach." She didn't know the date, but she did know it was the holiday of Pesach. There were no calendars, and the only shul in Shargorod was demolished at some point in 1942, so how people knew the dates for the holidays puzzles me. Still, some Jewish tradition was practised and the holidays of Purim, Yom Kippur and others were remembered and symbolically observed. Somebody must have found a way to keep track.

⁓

One day, I noticed that my uncle Armin, who lived nearby, was trying to learn Russian. I asked him why, since he was having so much trouble with it, and he said he would tell me when I was older. For the time being, he requested that I not ask any questions. The next day, he asked me to do something for him, but it had to be kept a big secret. That was fun!

There was a young woman with a baby in our hut. Uncle Armin had been building a wooden carriage to take the baby for walks. Somehow, he had managed to find four little wheels and wooden boards and after a few days, the carriage was ready. Uncle Armin and my parents asked me if I would take the baby out on the days when the weather was not too bad. The ghetto had a few streets on which we were allowed to walk. I was to push the carriage to the other end of our street, a walk of about twenty minutes. There, I was to meet a man with a brown cap and leave the baby and the carriage with him.

At first, I did this every few days. It was always the same routine – each time I would give the buggy to this man, a few hours later the baby was somehow back in the hut. I never saw who brought it back. Sometime later, I took the baby for these walks almost every day. I had promised Uncle Armin not to ask any questions and I was happy with the extra piece of bread I got when I returned from the walks.

Everything had a price. . . . Only a year later, after we had been liberated, did I find out that the carriage had a double bottom, where Uncle Armin hid all kinds of goods he had managed to steal from the soldiers' depot, like salt, lard, grenades, gunpowder, papers, and so on. When he disappeared from the shanty, Uncle Armin always said, "I have transactions to do." The man I left the baby with was a partisan, a resistance fighter, who took the loot into the woods where the partisans camped. I was very proud to have played a small part in helping the partisans in the forest. They were busy sabotaging the Romanians by blowing up bridges and roads so that ammunition and soldiers could not be transported to the front lines and wounded soldiers could not be transported to hospitals.

By the spring of 1944, there were rumours that the Axis forces were withdrawing. We didn't know when, as there were no newspapers or radios in the camp. In March, we heard cannons firing in the distance, and we knew that the front line was close. As the sounds got louder, Uncle Armin warned us to hide from the retreating German SS units – he was certain they would kill everybody before they withdrew, so as not to have witnesses to the crimes they had perpetrated. Uncle Armin told us to climb down to the potato cellar and dig a large hole so that we could hide there. It was very hard to move away all the earth the men dug out, but we all carried bundles of it to the pond when we went for the call of nature. Other survivors did the same thing, and we all planned to stay in the cellar until the Soviet army arrived.

Only eleven of us were left to hide in the potato cellar: my father and mother, my only surviving grandmother, two other deportees with a baby, Babushka's family of four, and me. We all squeezed into that hole. It was impossible to move and very difficult to breathe, even though my father removed a rock from a corner of the hole so we could get some air. It was a miserable, dark, musty, damp, cold hole. Mice and rats scurried between our feet. When the baby cried, the mother put a wet rag on his face to muffle the sound. From time to time one of the men climbed up to the hut to fetch one of the pails of water that we had brought from the dirty pond. The women had prepared these pails while the men dug the hole.

Through the hole where the rock was knocked out we could hear noises from outside: shots, stomping of heavy boots and loud German voices. We were terrified. My mother said, "We have struggled with death for so long, and now, when the ordeal is almost over, we could be murdered if the soldiers find us."

Suddenly, a burst of song, in Russian, erupted from the street. My father ordered us not to move in case it was a ploy by the retreating German Nazis to lure us out of hiding and murder us. A few hours later, Uncle Armin came in from his "transactions" and told us it was safe to come out. "The partisans are here!" he yelled exuberantly. We untangled our stiff, tired bodies, and cautiously climbed out of the hole. We could not believe that we were no longer captives. Ukrainian partisans, jumping up and down with guns in their hands, were singing Russian and Ukrainian songs of victory. To our surprise, the heroic partisans who had liberated us were mere boys and girls between fourteen and seventeen years old! These partisans had been too young to be mobilized into the Soviet army at the beginning of the war. Towards the end of the war, as they were older, members of the Communist Party indoctrinated them with communism and the goal to fight the fascist enemy by becoming partisans. A few Jewish youth who had managed to escape also joined the partisans in the forest, with the fascists as their common enemy. The partisans were not particularly motivated to save Jews, but if saving Jews happened to be a side effect of sabotaging the enemy, that was okay.

The kitchen staff was the last German SS unit to leave the front line through Shargorod. The partisans had managed to capture the cook, a tall blond fellow in his twenties. With his hands tied behind his back, he walked head down between two partisans much younger than he was. Suddenly, out of nowhere, low-flying German airplanes descended from the sky, spraying machine-gun fire at us, killing many. The cook raised his head and cried out, "Es kommt doch deutsche Hilfe!" (German help is on its way after all!) He had hardly finished his words when the partisans opened fire on him. Later, though he was long dead, every time a partisan passed by, he shot another bullet into the cook's body. About six hours later, the Soviet armies entered Shargorod. Had it not been for the young partisans, many of us might have been murdered just before we were liberated.

The Trek Back Home

As a naive, pampered and sheltered child, the only granddaughter to my grandparents and the only niece to my aunts and uncles, I had been completely unprepared for the perils that I had had to face at such a young age. The expulsion from school, the persecution, the forced abandonment of my home and birthplace, the atrocities that occurred on the deportation train, the horrors I witnessed during the night in the barn, the terrifying episodes in Ataki, that horrible barge, the three-day death march from Mogilev to Shargorod and the three days in the potato cellar – among many other experiences – stripped me of what little remained of my childhood.

Innocence was forever gone and my stability and anchor, my family, almost entirely obliterated. In total, I lost thirty-six members of my family in Transnistria. My uncle Armin had had eleven siblings; only three, including him, survived the Holocaust. His parents were also murdered. Most of my relatives who survived had suffered terribly. My beloved Omama had lost the knuckles on both her hands from gangrene. My parents, who survived physically, suffered from chronic depression that had started in Transnistria. This remained a constant with them for the rest of their lives. They were emotionally crippled and old before their time; I never saw them sing or dance again.

$\sim$

Before we embarked on yet another chapter of adversity, we remained in our shanties in Shargorod for several weeks, trying to regain some strength and decide what to do. Once somewhat revived, we started on our long trek home. Even though it was only about four hundred kilometres to Dorna, it took us more than a year to get there. Since all trucks and trains were being used for the war, we had to make our way on foot. This was extremely rough, given how little energy we had left to walk, and not having reliable food, water or a place to sleep.

We occasionally got a short ride from a passing truck or a peasant with a horse and a four-wheel cart. We ate what we could find in the fields or what some peasants gave us. The Soviets tried their best to assist by dropping from their low-flying planes cartons of black bread, chocolate and cans of caviar. While most people think caviar is a great treat, given that it is an expensive delicacy, it is terribly salty, and we had neither bread nor water to quench our thirst. Since that time, I cannot stand the sight of caviar.

The men, including my father and uncle, sourced the remaining food required for us to survive. I have absolutely no idea where they got it from. I was still a child, and wasn't told things like this. There was just enough sustenance to carry on, although we were always hungry. As we walked, unguarded, up and down the dirt roads, we went at our own pace, sleeping whenever we were tired, mostly in barns with the permission of the farmers.

When we were liberated, I hadn't realized I was in such bad shape. My spine had become deformed, curved from sometimes having to sleep on a cold, damp, dirt floor. My teeth were rotting, partly from malnutrition. Because food had been so scarce, for my thirteenth birthday the best gift I could wish for was a whole slice of bread! I called it, "All around the bread." I had huge gland-like cysts filled with pus under both of my arms, and smaller ones on other parts of my body, most likely from malnutrition and bacteria from eating dirty vegetables. My body was cleansing the junk in my system by developing boils with pus, and they hurt so much that for nearly a year I couldn't keep my arms by my sides; when walking I had to hold them up to avoid the excruciating pain. After we finally returned to Romania, a doctor cut the cysts open, drained the pus and sewed the skin back. I still have the scars, and they will be there until I die.

Since some parts of Romania had not yet been liberated, when we entered towns or cities where the Soviets and Germans were still fighting in the streets, we had to hide in ruins to avoid the bullets. It was hard to find water because many fountains had been poisoned. Most of the time we were just behind the front line, so we were exposed to shooting from both the ground and the air.

Finally, we reached the city of Czernowitz, the capital of the province of Bukovina. Many Jewish people had lived there before the war. There, we were told that Soviet soldiers were rounding up able-bodied men, herding them into trucks and driving them to the coal mines deep in the Ural Mountains to be used as slave labour. The irony, of course, was that we had been liberated by the Soviets, and now we were being hunted by them. I was totally puzzled by this strange turn of events. My father and Uncle Armin, recognizing the extreme danger of being captured, came up with a plan. They intended to drive to the city of Beltz, in the province of Bessarabia, in the hope that we could stay with my aunt Sidi and her family. Driving to Beltz meant having to make an enormous geographical detour from our route to Dorna.

However, we somehow found out that Aunt Sidi and her family had long ago taken refuge in Central Asia, in Uzbekistan. We later discovered that both her husband and baby boy were killed during the bombing of their train. Sidi had spent the war working in a factory in Tashkent, the capital of Uzbekistan. My father and uncle somehow sourced a truck and next decided to drive to Kishinev, another big city in Bessarabia (now Moldova), where we used to have some friends. Unfortunately, they too had been evacuated to Central Asia, so we had no option but to rent a room there. I ask myself where and how they got the money to rent a truck, buy gasoline, rent a room and buy food, but I never asked them while they were alive, so I have no idea. The landlady offered us a ground-floor room with one condition: since the door could only be accessed through another rented room, we had to promise to climb through the window when we had to enter or exit our room. We stayed there through the rest of the year, during the very cold winter months of 1944 and into the beginning of 1945.

As soon as the snow had thawed in the early spring of 1945, we again began our trek to Dorna, repeating a large part of our earlier route. By this point we were desperate to get home, hoping to find some of our relatives who had disappeared since the deportation. We finally got to our former home in Dorna on May 5, 1945, about fourteen months after our liberation. By that time, the military presence was gone. Any semblance of home before the war was gone, too. Our apartment had been completely plundered and looted. Everything had been stripped bare, including the chandeliers, crystals and carpets. Even the neighbours were different. Everything had changed.

Since our house was unique, having running water and a separate exit in every room, in 1941 it had become a German hospital where wounded German soldiers were treated alongside locals who were sick. When Romania was occupied by the Soviets in September 1944, it became a hospital for wounded Soviet soldiers; when we arrived, it had been transformed into a fire station.

On our return, the authorities gave us back one room on the second floor of our house. Another room on the ground floor was given to my grandmother, Omama Rebecca, because her little bungalow outside of town had been destroyed during the war.

The firemen did not treat us poorly, but they didn't concern themselves with our basic well-being, not even offering simple gestures like asking us if we had anything to eat. If it hadn't been for the stash my father had hidden in the attic, we would surely have been in dire straits. Luckily, the double wall my father had built before we were deported had remained intact. In exchange for a packet of needles – a valuable and scarce commodity at that time due to steel shortages – my father could easily get enough food to last us a few days or more. As far as the jewellery he had buried under a tree in the backyard, it may have been extremely helpful, but no one dared dig it up.

Several weeks after our return home, my forty-one-year-old father got a job in a lumber mill. My mother, now thirty-six, found an office job. After work she was extremely active in a Socialist-Zionist organization called Hashomer Hatzair. I too became involved with a Socialist-Zionist organization, Hanoar Hatzioni. I felt passionate about my involvement, but I also became very involved with the Union of Communist Youth. Now, for the life of me, I cannot understand how I simultaneously belonged to the Zionist organization. Yet, communist propaganda had a huge impact on me at that time, as it did for most youth who had lived through the war. After the atrocities we had witnessed, we readily welcomed the idealism of communism. We believed that communism was God's gift to the universe; with its lofty ideals of equality, fraternity and liberty, as in the French Revolution, we were enthralled by it, and most of my friends and I were members of the Communist Youth Party. After all, this political system was implemented in the Soviet Union, and they were the ones who had saved us. Little did we know how wrong we were – our reality quickly turned sour. I was so hooked on communism that I bought my mother a little gypsum bust of Stalin for her birthday. How could I have been so stupid?

My parents realized that there was still a lot of antisemitism in Romania and really no future for us there. They wanted to leave as soon as the authorities would provide travel visas. Those documents, however, were issued only intermittently, and there were times when no one was allowed to leave. In any case, due to my involvement with the communist youth group, I was against emigrating. My parents would not leave without me. I feel guilty to this day about that.

In September 1945, I went back to school, though it wasn't really a regular school. The instructors lumped students by their age and put them together in one room. I was placed in a higher grade than I should have been in, but they taught us very little anyway. Some kids even sat in the back row of the classroom playing poker while the teacher was talking. This school was equivalent to an elementary level; for example, one of the silly questions on the graduation exam was: "What is more, one hour and twenty minutes or eighty minutes?"

Unfortunately, there was no high school in Dorna. I knew so many people my age who wanted to go to high school, so I decided to organize one. I discovered an empty building in town and, with some money and workers from the city authorities, I managed to have it repaired – windows were fixed, missing door handles and light bulbs were replaced. I also bought mattresses for a dorm for children from the surrounding area. Only fourteen at the time, I then had to travel to Bucharest to get a permit from the Ministry of Education that would allow the school to function. I travelled with the support of the Communist Party and the youth organization; by that time I was a member of the Central Committee of the Union of Communist Youth, getting ready to become a "Future Communist Leader." I had to bring to the Ministry of Education lists of the names of all the children my age who needed high school, both Jewish and non-Jewish, and I had a list of prospective teachers. I took all this documentation to the ministry in Bucharest and applied for the permit. I had to stay in Bucharest for one week because of bureaucratic delays. My charming hostess for the week was none other than the Minister's secretary.

I got the permit, but, sadly, when I came back to Dorna, not one window was left in the building. Everything had been stolen – handles and doors, mattresses and kitchen equipment, even light bulbs. Nothing remained. In one week, the unsupervised building had been plundered. There was no way we could have a school now.

My parents decided to send me to Satu Mare, where my uncle Armin was born and where he and Aunt Mila had moved, so I could go to high school there. Satu Mare was a big city in the province of Transylvania. This city is well known in the Orthodox Jewish community for the famous rabbi, the Satmar Rebbe, who lived there and has a big following to this day.

I was cause for concern for my uncle and aunt. Even though I was not of marriageable age, I was very pretty when I was young, and they considered me competition for my uncle's older niece whom they wanted to marry off. When a prospective husband came to meet her at their house, I was not allowed to open the door, and I had to stay hidden in another room lest the suitor catch a glimpse of me. My uncle also needed to fend off the romantic, persistent boys from my school who came to the house to serenade me at night. When they showed up, my uncle would either spray them with soda water bottles or throw a whole pail of water on them so that they would leave us alone, even though I enjoyed the attention immensely.

I went to school in Satu Mare for two years until, in 1948, a high school finally opened in Dorna. I was still very active in the Communist youth organization during those high school years and, as a member of the central committee, I took my first two trips abroad. I was sent to Budapest, Hungary, and to Prague, in what was then Czechoslovakia, to liaise with our corresponding organizations. The best part of these trips was the sightseeing tours that my "comrades" took me on. In Prague we went to the Old Jewish Cemetery, one of the oldest in Europe, where the number of persons buried is uncertain because, due to lack of space, there are up to twelve layers of graves. I saw the grave of the sixteenth-century scholar Rabbi Judah Loew ben Bezalel who, according to legend, created the famous mythical Golem, a being made from clay, to protect Jews from antisemitic attacks in Prague.

Back in Dorna, I worked on some communist committee projects with a young man named Peter, a security officer in the communist system who was temporarily stationed there. He was very handsome, especially in uniform, and I had the pleasure of being the source of his attraction. My mother was terribly scared of him because of his role as a security officer, but Peter proved to be quite the gentleman when he generously offered us his own ration cards to supplement our meagre post-war rations.

In 1949, when I graduated from high school in Dorna, I was hoping to continue on to study medicine but Romania was beginning to institute a Five-Year Economic Plan wherein allocation for medical doctors and other professionals was extremely regulated, and the authorities had different plans for me. One of the priorities under communism was to replace French with Russian as the second language in schools. However, there was a lack of Russian teachers, so students who graduated from high school with the highest marks were carefully selected for training. I was one of them. Our teachers were brought from the Soviet Union to the Maxim Gorky Institute in Bucharest, a university campus dedicated to a four-year program of total immersion in the Russian language, literature and linguistics. Ironically, had my marks not been so high, I might have been able to go to medical school, as I had hoped, instead of studying Russian language and literature. Nevertheless, I enjoyed my studies and could hardly predict how knowing Russian would open so many other doors later in my life.

In Bucharest, I met up again with Peter, who had been transferred there. Although we met occasionally, we never had a romantic encounter. Over time, I became acquainted with his family. Later on, when my parents and I decided to emigrate, we stopped seeing each other, not only because it was too dangerous for him, but also because it was clear that there was no future between the two of us. Nevertheless, we promised to stay in touch.

In 1953, upon graduating from the Maxim Gorky Institute, I obtained the equivalent of a master's degree in Russian language and literature, with a minor in linguistics. I was immediately appointed as assistant to the professor of Russian language and literature. I lived in a dorm with three other female students a couple of years older than me. All my roommates smoked and, since I wanted to appear more mature, I began smoking too. I soon became addicted.

That year, my beloved Omama passed away and I had to travel to Dorna for her funeral. She had the "honour" of dying on the same day as Stalin, and everyone had to wear a black ribbon on the sleeve to mourn him. Since I did not have enough money for a train ticket, I travelled to Dorna on top of the train. As it sped through tunnels I had to lie flat on the roof, like in the movies, and when I arrived home, I had black soot all over my face and my clothes. I suppose that anyone seeing me walk the few blocks from the train station to our house thought I was a chimney sweep. My parents had a fit when they saw me.

After graduating and getting involved with the "real world," I began to realize that communism was not, in fact, a better system for the population. It was a good system only for those who were in the upper echelons of the Communist Party. My disillusion peaked when there were rumours that the Romanian currency was to be changed, and the politicians had us travel to different areas in the country and emphatically deny the rumours. A few days later, the currency was changed and people lost their savings.

Now totally disappointed in the system, I became very depressed. My parents had been cynical about the system since 1945, when they had wanted to apply for emigration and I had refused. As antisemitism intensified, I finally agreed that we should apply for an emigration visa, in spite of all the risks. At that time, applying to leave the country was very dangerous because you were immediately considered an enemy of the state and always fired from your job. The party mentality was, "If you are not with us, you're against us." By this point, around 1958, I was an editor of an excellent literary magazine in Bucharest and also worked part-time at the Institute of Linguistics, redeveloping a dictionary of the Romanian language. I was immediately dismissed from both of my positions. At the time I was dismissed the letter we had reached was "M" and the word we were working on was *mofluz*. Translated into English, it means "sourpuss."

To apply to leave the country with my parents, the applications had to be filed together, so I travelled back to Dorna. We had to stand in line for long periods of time at the City Hall to get the applications. To discourage and humiliate those of us waiting, the government ordered the firemen to attack us from time to time with powerful, high-pressure water hoses. Some people were even hurt from the water pressure, but no one left the line. When we finally stepped into the office, we were soaking wet.

By the time we applied, in early 1958, we had already remained in Romania for many years after the war, and my parents' health was in very poor condition. My mother's sister Sidi had returned from Uzbekistan and was already living in Israel. My father's sister, Etty, and her husband, Molly, who had lived in Dorohoi before the war and also survived the deportation to Transnistria, also managed to get to Israel.

I needed to help my parents with all the arrangements the government required in case our exit application was approved. These consisted of paying property taxes for five years in advance, painting the interior and exterior of the house, as well as making any necessary repairs, and paying in advance in case the sidewalk needed repairing in the next five years. All this was in order to comply with the Five-Year Economic Plan and, mostly, to harass the applicants.

While in Dorna, I met a former schoolmate, Lia, who worked in the library. She told me that she was working in a back room where she registered books. According to the Five-Year Economic Plan, she had to register three hundred books per month to get her full pay. I was very surprised that a town of several thousand people required that number of new books. Lia explained that the books were not new; they were being brought from a bunker where many books had been stored during the war. In my naïveté, I asked her what would happen when all these old books had already been registered. Lia replied, without blinking an eye, "We already had a meeting about this and decided to put them all back in the bunker and start registering them again." Needless to say, I was not impressed with the efficiency of the Five-Year Economic Plan. This encounter further reinforced my desire to get out of Romania.

However, no one got a permit to leave Romania simply because they applied, and actually receiving it was totally random. Exit documents were approved haphazardly – one just waited and hoped. We were all "enemies of the state," living in complete uncertainty. I have many friends whose applications to leave were refused until recently, and they had been living in Romania in miserable conditions.

It wasn't until the 1990s that I found out that Israel had entered into a treaty with Romania; it was a secret, informal agreement in the 1950s, but by the 1960s, Israel was paying Romania in hard currency for every person allowed to exit. The price per person fluctuated depending on age, education and state of health. It is interesting that Germany had the same deal with Romania: for every German allowed to leave Romania, the government received a certain amount of money. Ceauşescu, the communist president of Romania, used to say that the Jews and the Germans were his most valuable natural resources.

While we waited for our papers, my parents lived in Dorna and I returned to Bucharest, with no money to pay for rent or living expenses. Unfortunately, on my identity card the line indicating "profession" clearly stated that I had been the editor of a popular literary magazine, so when I applied for a job and showed my card, it was immediately clear that I was fired for "political" reasons. I experienced one rejection after another, even from simple jobs like cashier in a grocery store or as a salesperson. Secretarial work was out of the question, as I could not type.

Finally, I illegally changed my name to Felicia Costea, a Romanian name. Then, I wrote several interesting literary articles and published school books under this name. However, this was a very risky thing to do. For a while, my friends from the literary magazine gave me some proofreading and editing to do at home and they initialled each page for me. That lasted for two to three months, until I made a mistake in the translation of a quote by Lenin, of all things. My friends were interrogated and admonished for helping me, and I was penniless again.

Then, having no other choice, I took a job as a street sweeper, sweeping garbage in a certain area of Bucharest. I kept my sanity during this period by noticing everything going on in the neighbourhoods where I was working. Although I avoided speaking to people, I heard them discussing all sorts of things. After a few weeks, I knew who among the married residents in "my area" were having affairs with whom, what time the lovers were coming, who was physically abusing their spouse, who was cheating on the job by going to work after lunch instead of at 8:00 a.m., and so on. I kept myself preoccupied with these types of observations for some humorous relief. I had no intellectual involvement with anything or anybody during that time, so I fabricated it from what I saw around me.

A few months later, my life unexpectedly changed. The Ministry of Energy requested the collection of garbage samples in different areas of the city. Garbage sweepers were required to collect samples from their areas, place them in small, sterilized containers provided by the authorities and mark them with the date, time and place where they were collected. I wrote my labels legibly, nicely and neatly. This went on for several weeks and I had no idea what it was for, but you didn't argue and didn't ask questions of the authorities.

One day a middle-aged woman came by, introduced herself as Esther and stopped to talk to me. Esther told me that the Romanian government had decided to build facilities for heating student dorms by burning garbage. She was hired as a chemist for the laboratory and she researched the calories of heat generated by burning each of the three different types of garbage – agricultural, industrial and domestic.

Esther came by because my notes on the samples were very precise and the writing very schooled. During the conversation we realized that we were both Jewish, and I told her about my employment prior to applying for an exit visa. My ability to speak Russian and German was of use to her because her laboratory equipment came from those two countries and she couldn't read or understand the instructions for how to install and use it. At the end of our conversation, she asked me to work with her at the lab as her assistant. I had no knowledge of her chemical experiments, but she said she would teach me, and we shook hands.

Slowly, I learned a little chemistry and what buttons to push for this and that. After a few months, Esther's mother got very sick. Esther was her mother's only caregiver because none of her deported family members had returned from the camps. She was beginning to miss many hours of work to be with her mother. Then her mother was hospitalized, and Esther was gone from the lab for even more hours, and sometimes days. One day, in her absence, I pushed the wrong button and caused a small explosion that set my lab coat and one piece of equipment on fire. I was fortunate to get out, and I rolled in the grass to put out the fire on my back. But the smoke had wrecked the lab.

I was terrified for both of us about the punishment that awaited us. We could have been thrown into jail. After the incident, I did not hear from Esther directly, but one of her neighbours informed me by telephone that after the death of her mother, Esther had moved to a one-room apartment. Eventually, Esther phoned me to give me her new address and phone number. She had managed to explain the fire at the lab by signing a declaration that some equipment was faulty.

Instead of jail, I was sent to work on the outskirts of the city at the garbage dumps where toxic materials were shipped. The area was surrounded by white powder, possibly lime sulfur, to control funguses, pests and disease. So now I was working on trucks unloading garbage at the dump. I wore rubber boots up to my hips. During this time, I was sharing an apartment with a girlfriend on Calea Victoriei, Victory Avenue, a beautiful main street in central Bucharest. We shared the kitchen and the bathroom with a couple of gay opera singers.

At the dump, I was working with people who had various physical and mental problems. Many were injured, some were crippled, some alcoholics and some were Roma rejected by their tribe. That's the kind of crew, plus me, that the authorities put together to work in such a toxic place. We worked only seven hours a day instead of eight because it was a toxic environment. I wanted to do something for these other workers, so I organized literacy classes, and after work I taught them how to read and write. I don't know what possessed me to organize a literacy class. I think that, although I may not always be aware of it at the time, I try to find positive things in my life. It's either my nature to do so, or perhaps it's my philosophy of *tikkun olam*.

Nonetheless, this seven- or eight-month period was a horrible time in my life. I had nightmares of people following me home from the dumps. I would come home in the evening from work smelly and exhausted. I had made an agreement with the guys in our apartment that the bathroom would be free when I returned from work so I could go straight to the bathtub and soak. I had to get the dirt and smell off me. After the bath, I'd go to the opera. In communist countries all the arts were supported by the state, so tickets were very cheap. I went almost every night, and could sing every opera. Going to the opera so often kept me sane.

That job lasted until the day an incinerator in one of the city's hospitals malfunctioned. By law, hospitals were not allowed to send their garbage to public dumps and were instead supposed to dispose of it in their own incinerators. Because it had malfunctioned, I found myself unloading hospital waste containing all kinds of horrible things. I developed jaundice from that experience and couldn't go to work anymore. Once again, I didn't have money to pay rent.

Luckily, it was not long after this that we got our exit papers. Somehow, my family was fortunate, and our papers came through in the summer of 1959. They were to Cuba, but we decided to use the papers just to get out of Romania. Before leaving, everyone had to pay up the requirements I described earlier. That applied to my parents, who would be vacating their room, but not to me, since the apartment remained occupied. Since we needed money for these taxes, and we wouldn't be allowed to take many things with us anyway, I took the train back to Dorna and went to the flea market to sell things. I played my accordion there to attract more people. I don't remember selling anything other than the chewing gum I got from my aunt in Israel, but I must have sold other things because I earned enough money to pay the five-year advance for my parents' taxes. My parents also contributed whatever they could. Once we paid everything off and got rid of all our stuff, we were ready to leave.

That summer, immediately after receiving the exit certificates, we bought our train tickets, just in case the authorities changed their minds. Many of my colleagues from the literary magazine came to the station to say goodbye, as did Esther, meaning they put themselves in danger. Then, I never heard from them again. It was too risky for them to correspond with an "enemy" of the country.

Leaving Romania

We travelled by train to Vienna via Hungary. We were restricted to one suitcase per person and twenty-five family photographs. Despite these restrictions, I was determined to take a piece of contraband – a five-dollar bill sent in a letter from my aunt Mila; she had hidden it between two glued-together photographs and it had miraculously gone undetected. At that time, five dollars, especially American dollars, was considered a small fortune! A few hours into the trip I asked myself if it was worth the risk with the border guards and decided against it. I went to the toilet and left the pictures on top of the water cistern for some fortunate soul to discover. Although I'm gutsy in some things, when it comes to danger, I have no qualms in playing it safe.

On the seat directly across from us was an extremely obese Orthodox lady, wearing a *sheitl*, wig, and turban. When we came to the border with Hungary, the border guards searched everyone's luggage. They noticed that the lady was wearing a diamond earring in her left ear and demanded that she part with it but she refused, explaining that it was a precious heirloom from her grandmother. The train came to an immediate halt and remained in the station for nearly two hours while the border police continued bickering with her to remove her jewel. As the guards continued to insist, the lady became increasingly hysterical. Why the guards made such an effort to gain her consent was beyond us, given that they could have easily taken the earring from her simply by restraining her. Perhaps they wanted to demonstrate their power over her, with her screaming, crying and making such a huge scene. In the end, she had no choice but to relinquish the earring, and we moved on. When we arrived at the Vienna transit area, the lady went to the toilet and, after half an hour, to our delight emerged as a slender young woman, her *sheitl* and turban discarded. Her "fat" had consisted of several corsets stuffed with jewellery and dollars. As for the earring with its tiny diamond? It had been a decoy. I thought to myself, What a gutsy lady. And to think that I was so afraid to smuggle out five dollars!

In Vienna, we were greeted and thoroughly briefed by a group of energetic *shlichim*, Israeli immigration agents, who were trying to convince us to go to Israel. Although we had considered immigrating to Belgium, where my aunt Mila and uncle Armin were living with their daughter, Diana, who had been born in 1949, we also had family in Israel and, more importantly, Zionism had become the new source of my idealism. We chose Israel.

In July 1959, we flew to Israel, arriving at 5:00 a.m. At the airport, we learned that standard procedure was to send all newcomers who didn't speak Hebrew directly to an *ulpan*, Hebrew language classes, for three to four months. These classes, however, had already begun in June, so the authorities wanted to send us to a hotel until September, when new classes would start. I was very disappointed and frustrated. I tried to convince them to send my family to an *ulpan* midstream, since we already had some basic Hebrew, but they refused. Their inflexibility made me even more frustrated and angry, so much so that I refused to budge from the airport. I knew that Hebrew was critical to landing a job in Israel, and the delay of months was out of the question. What did they expect? That I would sit in a hotel all day long with my parents twiddling my thumbs until classes started up again? No way. Not me. I was such a nuisance that by 5:00 p.m. they put us in a taxi, registered for an *ulpan* in Nazareth.

Although the classes were already one month underway, I quickly caught up. Not so with my parents. Grasping the language proved to be a major barrier for my parents, particularly for my father, who was not much of a conversationalist to begin with. Living conditions were harsh: we lived in small, shed-like tin houses that became extremely hot under the relentless Mediterranean sun. But most difficult of all was the uncertainty of our new lives in this strange and unfamiliar land.

After completing the *ulpan*, I secured a job at Histour, a tourism agency, in Tel Aviv. Naturally, because I spoke several different languages, they wanted me to work with tourists who spoke the languages that I knew well. But my preference was to work with Israelis, not foreign tourists, since I desperately wanted to advance my Hebrew, and so I demanded that I be transferred to work with Israelis leaving for abroad instead. My determination and ability to negotiate paid off and I was eventually assigned work with Israelis, just as I had hoped. Learning to work in a foreign language required a good sense of humour. One day, I followed up on a delay in the stamping of some passports I had forwarded to the Tourism Ministry. When I called the Ministry and asked them about it, I confused the words *darkonim*, passports, with *tachtonim*, underwear. As you can well imagine, asking officials out loud where my underwear was (*eifo hatachtonim sheli?*) resulted in an office bursting with laughter to the point of near hysteria. It was quite an embarrassing moment!

While I stumbled my way through Hebrew, Israelis struggled with my German-sounding last name, Steigman. No matter how hard they tried, they simply couldn't seem to pronounce or write it. So I decided to change it – simple as that. One Saturday, en route to see my aunt Sidi, who was living near Haifa, I made a small detour to the magnificent hanging gardens of the Bahá'í Temple on Mount Carmel. I was so enthralled by the beauty of the mountain that I instantly decided to become a Carmelly ("my Carmel") and kept that last name from then on. I had to go to an office and legally change my name, but there was no hassle there, since newcomers were encouraged to take on Hebrew names.

Israeli immigration policy did try to make some things easier for newcomers. For example, my having a university degree meant that my parents and I received a lovely two-bedroom apartment, in my name, in Rehovot, forty-five minutes away from where I worked in Tel Aviv. The commute by bus from our apartment to the tourist office was unbearably hot and time-consuming, so I began seeking other job opportunities closer to home. With persistence, I eventually found a position at the prestigious Weizmann Institute in Rehovot. Although I had no science background, I was able to translate research documents since I had a strong command of a few languages, and Russian was commonly used in scientific research at that time.

Around this time, I met up again with Marcel, an attractive man with whom I had collaborated back in Bucharest when organizing Romanian folk dancing and folkloric band competitions. He was your typical European Don Juan, a part-time film producer who also managed to find the time to play drums for a contemporary band. Marcel and I had lost contact for a few years, so when someone told me he was in Israel I was quite surprised. The last time I had seen him, I was working at the literary magazine, and he had come by to ask for a small bottle of liquid to remove ink from paper. I assumed he was using it to falsify documents. He disappeared soon after that and I was certain that he had ended up in jail. In fact, quite the opposite had happened. With his falsified documents, he had managed to get himself out of Romania and into Israel.

It didn't take long for us to begin dating. He was classy and incurably romantic and pretty much swept me off my feet. Boy, could we dance! Could he sing! He had a wonderful sense of humour and there wasn't a moment that he didn't have me smiling at some funny comment he'd made. And it seemed as though each time we met he had a bouquet of flowers for me. He was never afraid to take a risk and, although he gambled, I accepted it as an integral part of him.

Unfortunately, during this period, my mother and I were not getting along. In 1960, when Marcel asked me to marry him, I was quite open to it. Even though my head was in the clouds with Marcel, when it came down to it I was a practical kind of person, and I calculated that by marrying Marcel and having a family of my own I could secure a new apartment and be independent from my parents. When we married, Marcel agreed to take on my last name, Carmelly, without any fuss. I so much wanted to keep the name Carmelly, imagining that one day we would have a daughter whom I could name Jordana Carmelly, reflective of my full love for the Israeli land – encompassing both the largest river running through it, Jordan, and the most beautiful mountain, Carmel.

Shortly after we married, Marcel and I moved into an apartment in Tel Aviv, where I finally secured a job in my profession, teaching Russian at Bar Ilan University. I was so happy. I loved my work and loved the life I was leading. As for living in Israel, it was like living in the eye of a tornado – dynamic, exciting, always in motion – and it suited my temperament immensely. I experienced a freedom I had never felt before in my life, and I loved it. Strange as this might sound, it was the only place where, for the first time, I didn't feel Jewish. I was just like everyone else and I thrived because of it.

I travelled with my family to every corner of this magical country, including to kibbutz Ein HaShofet, where my cousin Ya'akov Shofar (previously Shufer) and his wife, Tzila, lived with their six children. With each new expedition I felt more and more at home and, in no time, I felt like I had always been an integral part of the Israeli culture.

I had so fully embraced the country that I completely internalized Hebrew as a language I could call my own. One day I was on the bus going to visit my aunt Sidi in Kiryat Bialik, a suburb of Haifa. I was reading Leon Uris's *Exodus* in Romanian and had absent-mindedly placed my thin bus ticket somewhere between its many pages. When the inspector came to check tickets, I couldn't find mine anywhere. Without a ticket, he insisted that I get off, but having just paid for my ticket, I refused. We both got very angry and, without realizing it, I began arguing with him in fluent Hebrew. While arguing, my book dropped to the floor and the ticket fell out. When I arrived at my aunt's house and told her the story, we were both very proud and pleased that I had finally become a true Israeli citizen.

The only problem I was having was that my mother was against my marriage to Marcel. "He doesn't have a reliable profession and he is such a floo-floo character," she said disapprovingly, even without knowing that he also gambled, or as Marcel referred to it, "free-lanced." Plagued by various chronic illnesses acquired in Shargorod, suffering from the heat, unable to master the Hebrew language, incapable of finding employment – and now, having a son-in-law they disapproved of – this was too much for my parents to handle. They decided to leave Israel and immigrate to Canada, where my aunt Mila and uncle Armin had settled after leaving Belgium.

I decided it would be best if we joined them. My rationale for immigrating to Canada with my parents was twofold. Firstly, I still felt incredibly guilty that my parents had remained in Romania for so long because of me; second, I was hoping that the move would help Marcel detach from his gambling group and that he would take the opportunity to find steady work in a new atmosphere. In 1961, Aunt Mila and Uncle Armin sponsored us to come to Canada. They were living in Montreal and their family had grown – I now had another cousin, Murray, who had been born in 1953. The Treisers were already well-established and Uncle Armin promised to give my father a job in his sportswear factory.

We arrived in Montreal in the spring of 1962. I had no idea that there were schools for learning English or assistance from the government to find employment there, though I am not sure if we would have been entitled to such services, given that we were sponsored by and lived with my aunt and uncle. After a disappointing job search, I found a position sweeping the floor at a hairdressing salon. Sweeping didn't turn out to be too bad an option for me as a first job in a new country. After all, I couldn't speak English and I did have experience sweeping.... Not long after that I began working for a dressmaker, sewing on buttons.

Television became my first English teacher and best friend. It was a great way to familiarize myself with both Canadian culture and the English language, although I must admit that it was not all that interactive. As soon as I met new Canadian friends, I wholeheartedly welcomed their invitation to play Scrabble, which proved to be an invaluable tool in helping me acquire the language skills I so desperately wanted.

As desperate as I was to learn the English language, I was also desperate to have a child. To my dismay, I couldn't get pregnant because one of my ovaries was completely dysfunctional and the other one was not that healthy either. I wondered if this was a consequence of all that I had been through as a young girl, such as sleeping on the cold dirt floor in Transnistria. To become fertile, I subjected myself to painful treatments, to no avail. Worse yet, Marcel found new gambling buddies in Montreal and my married life hit a wall. My anxiety spun completely out of control on both accounts.

In 1963, over the course of a few months, our marriage unravelled and, feeling completely hopeless, I decided to leave Marcel. I moved in with friends who had lived with us for several months when they first immigrated to Montreal. By then, we already had our own apartment. Two months later, I was alarmed as well as happy to find out that I was pregnant with Marcel's child! I couldn't bear the thought of being a single mother, so after Marcel's renewed promises that he would give up gambling for good, I moved back in with him.

I had an extra-uterine pregnancy, which was high risk. Without any awareness of the difficulties to follow, I experienced the rest of my term carefree, but on August 1, 1964, my baby was born by Caesarean section, prematurely, at only seven and a half months. She weighed a mere three pounds and had to stay in the hospital in an incubator for five weeks and be fed intravenously. I was completely anxious. The baby was too small and too weak for her lungs to function properly; she could only breathe through her mouth. Before the baby was born, we had decided that if it was a boy, we would name him after Marcel's father, who died before Marcel's bar mitzvah, and if it was a girl we would name her after my beloved grandmother, Omama Rivka. However, the pediatricians advised us to hold off on the baby-naming since there was a good chance that she would not survive, as premature babies often did not at that time.

Three nights after the birth, when I was still in the hospital, my Omama came to me in a dream and said, "I just found out that you had a little girl. Give her a name and don't worry. I will take good care of her." Marcel was in my hospital room when I woke up in the middle of the night crying, and I shared my dream with him. At 9:00 a.m. my aunt Mila phoned me and reiterated the same prophetic vision. "I dreamed about my mother last night. She told me that you should give the baby a name and that she would take care of her." We were totally blown away by this. I immediately rolled my wheelchair to the incubator to see the baby, while Marcel went across the street for a strong morning coffee to keep his nerves still. On his way, he saw a rabbi and stopped him to tell him the story about our baby and the dream. The rabbi looked him straight in the eyes and told him to go to the synagogue and give the baby a name right away. That very afternoon, Marcel went to a synagogue and gave our daughter the Hebrew name Rivka, after my grandmother, and the English name Ramona Joy. I chose the name Ramona because it reminded me of Romania and Joy because my Yiddish name is Freida, which means joy. From that moment on, there was a daily improvement in the baby's health, although she still remained confined to the incubator.

After five weeks, they finally let me take my baby home. She was still so tiny that I could hold her entire body in the palm of my hand. By that time, she had been so conditioned to breathing through her mouth that when it came time to feed her, she stopped breathing altogether. Her feeding was not an issue in the hospital because in the incubator, Ramona was fed through a tube, but at home feeding her by bottle was agonizing if not impossible – she would stop breathing, turn blue and make choking sounds. The only way that I could resuscitate her was by placing her in a pail of cold water followed by a pail of hot water or, alternatively, by pricking her with needles. She stopped breathing one to three times during each feeding. Imagine my agony feeding her day and night, every three hours! I thought that I would go completely mad.

At about six months, Romy's condition finally stabilized, which was an incredible relief. She was an extremely cute and outgoing infant. But Marcel's gambling continued and my home life did not improve. In 1966, when Romy was two and half years old, I decided to leave the marriage once and for all. When Marcel and I divorced, I was so ahead of my time that I had a divorce party at a restaurant in celebration and invited all of our friends. Marcel and I did this together, mind you, since we decided to remain friends for the sake of our daughter, but since it was my idea, Marcel thought it best that I pay for it. After I paid the tab, Marcel suggested that we all go to another restaurant for dessert, this time on him. To my surprise, he paid the bill. However, the police soon showed up at the restaurant because he had paid with a bad credit card. If this didn't confirm that I was doing the right thing in divorcing Marcel, I don't know what would.

I raised my daughter as a single parent. Marcel eventually moved somewhere out west, and as far as financial support from him, we never saw any. He clearly had no desire to take on any responsibility for her upbringing. Besides the luxuries that he lavished upon her on his three visits to Toronto when we lived there, we saw no interest in her well-being. Had he ever asked if she had enough money for the basics in life like food, or money for her Jewish education?

By this time, I had already picked up a fair amount of English from all of the soap operas I had watched, the endless games of Scrabble I had played and the countless number of words I had looked up in my dictionaries. I could hardly say that I was fluent in the language, but my imperfect English came in most handy. We had a friend who owned a large factory for aluminum doors and windows and always hired new immigrants, especially from Romania, where he too was from. He and his wife were part of my close circle of friends and also happened to be Romy's godparents. Of all the things that he could have offered me as a job, I was most surprised when he suggested I teach *English* to a group of his workers! He sent small groups of people to my house and I taught them elementary English while taking care of my baby. The more I taught, the more I learned. Soon I became a skilled English teacher, having never taken a single English class in my entire life!

Some funny incidents happened along the way because of my "expertise" in English. When I saw fitted bedsheets for the first time in my life at a neighbour's house, I was very excited because I had never seen anything like them in Romania. I was determined to buy a set of my own, and after I had saved up just enough from my English classes, I went to Eaton's to buy a full set of blue sheets. That is when my English was blown to smithereens. I had already practised my request in English with my neighbour before heading downtown, but by the time a saleslady asked me if I needed help, I said, "Yes, I need blue shitted feets." She blushed and, after a deep breath, asked me what I needed them for. Puzzled, I said, "To put on bed." She smiled sweetly, took me by the hand and led me to the bed linens department.

Despite my obvious failure at Eaton's, I was proud of myself when I went to the butcher and clearly expressed, in English, my desire for liver from the baby of the cow. He immediately understood that I wanted veal liver. Encouraged by this, I proceeded to a grocery store, asking for "sour milk" instead of buttermilk. I realized that I must have said something wrong when the owner turned to me, slightly offended, and said condescendingly, "Madam, we don't sell sour milk." My worst mistake was buying a can of meatballs for dogs because they were so cheap. Since European pets ate only leftovers from the table, I had no idea that in Canada there are cans of pet food in the stores. They were delicious, mind you.

These incidents only helped fuel the fire of my determination to improve my English. I spent hours reading the newspaper, with dictionaries on both sides of me. I would underline every word that I didn't understand and look each and every one of them up no matter how long it took. With my English proficiency improving, I felt I was ready to enhance my career. Since my dream of medical school was out of the question for someone my age, as I could no longer embark on such a long-term educational commitment, I decided, in 1967, to apply to the School of Social Work at McGill University. McGill recognized my degree from Romania, so instead of four years of study, I had only two years remaining to achieve my master's degree. Even though I failed the language part of the entrance exam, the dean was willing to take a chance on me. His bet was on the right student. I persevered and did so well that at the end of my first year, I received an award for excellence.

There were two incidents during my fieldwork at McGill worth mentioning. The first was when I was assigned to counsel a man who had fallen off a roof and broken his back. When I took down his date of birth and other intake information, I discovered that he was a Nazi during the war. There was no way that I could help this man. When I went to my supervisor to be relieved of the case I was shocked by her insistence that, to become a social worker, I had to counsel him. It wasn't until I went directly to the Dean of Social Work that my supervisor's decision was overturned and the client was assigned to someone else. To think that such a man was free to live in Canada and that my supervisor did not understand the impact of this blatant reminder of the terrible things that had happened to my family during the war!

The other incident was when I successfully negotiated funds for immigrant children. At one point during my training, I worked at a community centre with immigrant preschool children who were terribly disadvantaged because they couldn't speak English. After applying to the Ministry of Education for funds to teach these children English, I was told the Ministry had run out of money. One of the secretaries informed me on the sly that the department for the mentally handicapped had money, so I applied there. The challenge lay in how to position the case to get funding for the children who were clearly not mentally handicapped. I argued that although the children were not mentally challenged per se, without the language ability and the funding to help them with their English, they were in fact being handicapped or would end up that way as a consequence of educational negligence. The funds were, in effect, a preventive measure. Perhaps it was my persuasiveness or perhaps the Ministry simply needed an excuse to spend the funds in order to maintain their level of funding for the next year; whichever it was, we received the financial support and I felt very proud of myself. I fight for things that I believe in, but I don't hesitate to give up when I think it is a waste of my energy. I want to win the war but have no interest in the battle.

In 1969, after completing my master's degree in social work at McGill, I started working at the Baron de Hirsch Institute, now known as Jewish Family and Child Services. During this time, there was a large influx of Jews from Morocco, Algiers and Tunisia. Since I spoke French, I did a lot of work at the Institute with this population. Although I knew their language well, I knew nothing about their cultural habits or their traditions.

I soon realized that the young women were in dire need of education about contraception and early childhood education. Despite having had five or six children, these women experienced many challenges in taking care of their babies born in Canada. In their countries it was customary that their own mothers, not they, were responsible for raising the children, and since they had left behind their parents to immigrate to Canada, they had left behind their sole caregiving support as well. For these young women then, the thought of giving birth to a sixth child in Canada was frightening due to their lack of experience. Also, many of these couples decided not to have any more children in Canada, opting instead to work and improve their lifestyle by buying the things they could never have imagined owning in their own countries. But they knew nothing about birth control and were desperate to find out what to do.

So I was assigned to educate these women about birth control. For this purpose, I ordered a kit from Johnson & Johnson that included a variety of birth control methods, but I was soon reprimanded for it by the director of the Institute. When I was summoned to his office, he had the kit open on his desk and scolded me by saying, "Felicia, you should know better than to order such private materials to the Institute. This must never happen again."

The women's group immediately rejected all birth control methods I showed them, including birth control pills. In their culture, a woman took pills only if she was in severe pain or seriously ill. With such cultural constraints, I wracked my brain to try to figure out what would work best with these women. I started calling birth control pills *bonbons de bébés*, candy for children, and lo and behold, they went on the pills. I also figured out how to get them to use condoms. To give you an idea of just how much they were in need of education, one day, I came across one of these young women sitting on a bench in the park actually knitting a condom from macramé!

On behalf of the Institute, I was also challenged with teaching sex education to religious Jewish youth. I was responsible for organizing a Family Life and Sex Education Program in several modern orthodox Talmud Torah schools in Montreal, where some of the teachers were conservative-minded rabbis. To implement this program, I developed a curriculum, interviewed about thirty lay volunteers and selected fifteen for a training program I designed before they began to work with me. The program was specifically geared towards the Grades 5 to 7 students, boys and girls, who were reaching puberty. Before we began teaching in the classrooms, we had several sessions with the parents and the teachers, excluding the rabbis, in order to deal with concerns openly and ensure that everybody was on board ahead of time. We also tried to take into account the sensitivity of the rabbis. When we had to carry charts of male and female sex organs through the halls of the schools, we noticed the rabbis turning their heads away or covering their eyes in embarrassment. After that, we hid the charts in big, dark plastic bags.

Although we realized that we needed to be more discreet in how we handled sex education with the Orthodox, we also realized that we couldn't shy away completely from the subject matter. One day, I followed closely behind two students who were leaving school after the program, as I happened to be walking in the same direction as they were. I overheard them talking about the program. One of them told the other, "It was interesting to learn about that mensturbation." I realized then that we needed to tweak the program to ensure that certain critical words be written on the blackboard rather than simply taught verbally. With these minor adaptations, the program proved to be a success even with the religiously observant Jews. Recently, as I was writing about this chapter in my life, I thought that not many people would believe it. However, to my delight and surprise, I met a woman in Toronto who remembers having participated in this program as a student.

Independence

In 1970, I received a scholarship from the Allied Jewish Community Services to attend a Jewish leadership program at the Jewish Institute of Religion's School of Jewish Communal Service in Los Angeles. This Institute prepares people for leadership positions in the Jewish community; another branch of the school trains Reform rabbis. It was a scholarly, prestigious program, requiring a master's degree and distinction in work and community leadership to be accepted, so I was honoured to be considered. Although a relatively short program, requiring two summers to complete, it was quite intense. As much as I loved the intellectual rigour of the program, I enjoyed even more the attention I received for being the only Canadian and woman in a class of twenty-five male students, all from the United States. I was always considered an equal, yet I still stood out as a woman and the men treated me as such, which was nice given my recent divorce.

However, my situation was more challenging than if I'd simply been the carefree, independent woman I so longed to be at that time. I had left Romy in my parents' care back home, and my ex-husband, who still lived in Montreal at this point, was interfering with our agreed-upon childcare arrangements. When I called home to speak to my parents that first summer, I found out that my ex had requested Romy on more occasions than we had agreed to, often at inappropriate times, and I felt very vulnerable and upset. Even worse, after the first term ended, Marcel suddenly felt it was his right to step in after being an absent parent, which created a huge conflict between us. I decided to take Romy with me to Los Angeles the following summer despite the difficulty this would entail for me. In order to do that, I had to arrange full-time help, including both daycare during the day and babysitters for my late evening classes. This was quite an expensive added burden, but I saw it as necessary. I was so grateful to the teachers who generously helped me out with arrangements, as this was not an easy thing for me to manage from a distance.

Childcare arrangements are never effortless; just as everything was in order for departure, the daycare confirmation did not come through in time for us to catch the plane we were booked on. This proved to be a godsend. The flight plan of the plane was from Montreal to Toronto and from Toronto to Los Angeles. Luckily, I was able to book a later flight that same day. We took a taxi from the airport directly to the university, where there was a welcome party for us, and were quite surprised by the "welcome" we received on arrival. As we stood at the door with our suitcases in hand, people looked at us in shock, as if we were ghosts. As far as they knew, we were supposed to have been on the earlier plane – a plane that had crashed when landing in Toronto!

Though I was not a stay-at-home mom and Romy did not have a dad in the traditional sense, the childcare she received in Los Angeles during the remainder of my program was hardly inadequate. Next to our residence lived a lovely young American couple. Diana, a stay-at-home wife, was a godsend of a babysitter for Romy. Diana took Romy splashing and playing in the pool practically every day; she played with her at every opportune moment and in every respect loved my daughter dearly. The "summer vacation" in California with Diana was exactly what Romy needed.

After experiencing my first dose of independence in L.A., coming back to Montreal seemed difficult. While away I realized that I had never truly separated from my family and had never really had a chance to form my own identity. I was extremely close to my aunt Mila and uncle Armin Treiser in Montreal. They were the social hub of the family and my life, always introducing us to their friends, taking us with them to any and every social affair, and celebrating all of the holidays with us. But they were so well known in Montreal that nobody in their social circles even knew my name. Everywhere I went, people would refer to me as "the Treisers' niece." I felt more like an appendage to them than a person in my own right. It was affecting my sense of identity to such an extent that when I was offered a counselling position at Jewish Family and Child Services in Toronto, I readily accepted it. In 1972, I packed up and left with my daughter.

My family wasn't that upset that I was leaving. Marrying the Jewish gambler was one thing, but now I was involved with Alan, a man who was not even Jewish. This was such an affront to my family who had survived the Holocaust that they refused to acknowledge the relationship in any way. In reacting to my choices, my parents became so strong in their position about being Jewish that, in their desperation to preserve our Jewish continuity, they decided to move back to Israel. My aunt and uncle's reaction was more reserved, but they too were clearly upset. They were quite religious and also felt uncomfortable being around Al. This had never been my intention. I was very much attached to Al, a kind and special man, and felt I had the right to live my life independently and make choices that would make me happy, particularly when it came to my private life. So I stopped going to family events to which he was not invited and left with him and Romy for Toronto.

Before moving to Toronto, I had the opportunity to travel to Romania. A friend of mine had plans to go and, because he didn't speak the language, he offered to pay for me to come along so that I could help with any translation needed. Before we left, I contacted the Romanian Ministry of Education, and I arranged to speak to someone about including Holocaust education in the school system. When the plane landed in Bucharest, we disembarked to an intense display of airport security – a runway full of armed soldiers with cocked guns. The next morning, I went directly to the Ministry, where I was greeted most enthusiastically. However, nothing came out of those meetings and discussions. I travelled with my friend for the remaining two weeks. The thing that struck me most as we travelled throughout the country was that, in the midst of all of the beautiful places I saw and hospitable people I met, I passed statue after statue honouring Marshal Antonescu, the orchestrator of Jewish pogroms and deportations from Romania. This bothered me tremendously and I felt a strong need to immerse myself in something Jewish, so I made my way to Bucharest's majestic Temple Coral synagogue. I was saddened to learn that this beautiful synagogue had been ransacked by the extreme right Legionnaires in a pogrom in January 1941. Although it had been partially restored after the war with funds provided by the American Jewish Joint Distribution Committee, only a handful of Jews attended services there.

~

When we moved to Toronto, I had only five thousand dollars to my name. I used this as a down payment, purchasing a townhouse on Rusty Crescent off Van Horne Avenue in a new development in the Don Mills area. Al had secured a position at the Toronto YMCA.

In Toronto at that time, there was a sudden influx of Jews from Montreal, anglophones who felt they no longer had a place in Montreal with Quebec threatening to separate from Canada, so we were not a complete oddity. When I walked around the neighbourhood with Romy, people would often stop and talk to me. I found it very funny when they tried to pinpoint whether or not I was Jewish, inevitably turning the conversations to gefilte fish or something of that nature to ascertain my background.

As far as caregiving was concerned, Al proved to be the best surrogate father I could hope for. He taught Romy so many important things, such as how to swim. Also, our moral values were completely aligned and he was excellent at providing Romy with an ethical direction, teaching her the distinction between right and wrong. This turned out to be sadly ironic, since after two years in Toronto, he left me for a younger woman. Romy and I suffered terribly when Al left. It was very hard on me to turn into a single mother again, and I cried for days. But I had to get over it; I was determined that, despite everything, I wouldn't go back to Montreal. I had to make it on my own.

Though I was a single mom with a minimal income level, I considered private Hebrew school for Romy a necessity despite the extremely high fees. Romy had started in Jewish kindergarten and elementary school in Montreal. After our move to Toronto, she went to Bialik Hebrew Day School and the Community Hebrew Academy (CHAT), both excellent schools. We had no family or close friends in Toronto who were interested in Judaism or bothered to observe the Jewish holidays. In the absence of a Jewish milieu, the Hebrew school seemed a small price, which I was willing to pay.

I hadn't expected that Romy would experience difficulties at Bialik, but she was completely different from the other kids, and they let her know it. Most of them were from well-established, wealthy Canadian families, while she was, culturally, from an immigrant home. Whereas the other kids got tuna, salmon or cheese sandwiches for lunch, Romy got the leftovers from last night's dinner. The kids downright bullied her, taunting her by calling her lunch of stuffed cabbage "hippopotamus guts." Imagine how she must have felt when I made her a graduation dress from scratch when the other mothers were letting their daughters pick out the dress of their choice at specialty stores! I did not find out about the bullying until much later and felt so badly that she had endured this on her own. I knew that she loved the school and the teachers, but as for socializing, she had been ostracized.

The hardest discrepancy for Romy to bear between our home and others was the panic, frustration and anger that she was exposed to compared to the other children in their normal, comfortable, well-established homes. Having witnessed the hardships of my parents and experienced them myself, I was suffering from post-traumatic stress. Moreover, with so little money to my name when we first arrived in Toronto, money that was quickly invested in the townhouse, I was panicked by my lack of financial security, dependent as I was on my private practice and my job to keep us going. There was many a day that Romy took the brunt of my anger at the world, being the closest person to me at that time. While Romy partly understood what I was going through, she was too young to feel anything but resentment for me.

When I look back now, I certainly didn't spend as much quality time with Romy as I should have, or as I wanted to. With so much financial responsibility on my plate, I felt extremely lucky that she was an excellent student and relieved that I didn't need to worry about her academically. Since she was so bright, everything seemed to come naturally to her. She was also a born artist and thrived whenever she acted, sang or danced. I can still picture her in her room, spending hours rendering the most beautiful pointillist paintings.

Romy and I lived in the Don Mills area from 1972 to 1975. Since Romy was studying at Bialik Hebrew Day School, which was not close by, it was critical for me to find a small house in that neighbourhood so that I could commute from work to home and to her school easily. A real estate agent found a perfect little bungalow to meet our needs: it was built in 1940 and had two tiny bedrooms, a hall and kitchen, a finished basement, and an auxiliary little building in the back of the yard that had accommodated an auto mechanic's workshop.

My house was and is my temple. As a single mother and immigrant, I was pretty proud of myself for owning my own house. The little bungalow was perfect for the two of us, and its location was perfect, too, nestled in the centre of the Jewish community and surrounded by five synagogues, which offered interesting intellectual and spiritual stimulation, as well as proximity to Romy's school and my work.

To my great disappointment, Jewish Family and Child Services did not have the funds to cover the position for which they had hired me, even though they had pre-paid for my move to Toronto. So I was temporarily put in charge of the volunteer department, at a lower pay. I resented that and left the agency.

In 1977, I was offered an opportunity that sounded too interesting to pass up. It was a three-week project in which the Ontario Ministry of Education was sending a doctor, a social worker and a nurse to visit several Aboriginal reserves north of Thunder Bay to evaluate the social, medical and educational services there. I was asked to join the group as a social worker. I knew that I was the perfect fit for this position, but I had to consider Romy's needs as well. She was only thirteen at the time, and since I had no family in Toronto to leave her with, and my friends were all working, I asked the Ministry if I could take her with me. Permission was granted. I went to Romy's school to advise the principal that she would be absent for three weeks and asked if the teachers would be kind enough to give her supplementary homework. Taking Romy out of school to visit "Native reserves" did not sit well with the principal. When I told him about my plans, he looked at me like there was something wrong with me and refused to approve of her absence. I was very disappointed, but decided that my daughter's education was my responsibility. I was not asking the school for approval, just the homework, and I knew that the exposure to the reserves would be excellent for my daughter's education. So I packed our suitcases and we left.

We flew from Toronto to Thunder Bay, where we saw several billboards stating, "We love our Indians" and "Our Indians are precious to us" – both of which we found very patronizing. After one night at a hotel, which had a huge hall richly decorated with Aboriginal art and an enormous fireplace in the centre of it, we were transported by helicopter to a deep forest where the first reserve was located. This was the only means of transportation to and between the reserves, as there were no roads or runways for a plane to land.

We were housed in a community centre where there were several beds to accommodate people who might be sick. However, there were no doctors in the area, nor, apparently, any patients, as the beds remained unoccupied.

We visited the schools, with girls and boys in separate buildings. A woman was teaching the girls how to do intricate and beautiful beadwork, while a man was teaching the boys complicated sculpting in leather and wood. We thought that these were extracurricular activities, but to our surprise we discovered that this was the entire extent of the curriculum. There was absolutely no academic instruction whatsoever, even for the basics in reading, writing or math. I fervently jotted this observation down for our final report. When we went to other reserves I was alarmed to find out that this schooling was the norm.

I couldn't get over how appalling conditions were on the reserves. Surely someone could change how things were being handled! I wonder how much has changed since then. The protests and demonstrations that the First Nations people are staging today are not surprising given the long history of ongoing neglect, as well as our government's impositions, which makes them unable to manage their own affairs.

Upon our return home, Romy resumed school and I frantically worked on a full report for the Ontario Ministry of Education. It probably ended up on some bureaucrat's desk somewhere, never to be read. We were never contacted for the follow-up evaluation that had been budgeted for with taxpayers' money. Needless to say, the experience was eye-opening for both me and Romy. Not your typical trip for two nice Jewish girls.

Soon after this, I found a temporary counselling position at Jewish Vocational Services (JVS), a non-sectarian agency, where I spent the next two years replacing someone on maternity leave. After JVS, I was hired as the Director of Project Isaiah, a pilot project for all Reform congregations across Canada and the US. Its purpose was to find better ways to utilize Reform temples, which were mostly used on Shabbat and the Jewish holidays and for life-cycle events like weddings, baby namings and bar and bat mitzvahs. Through Project Isaiah the Reform temple was to be transformed into a community centre, and I was responsible for organizing different activities to meet the needs of various age and ethnic groups. I coordinated premarital training; weekly get-togethers for seniors, the recently married, and singles groups; and Bible study for young mothers, as well as daycare for their babies and toddlers.

I worked at Holy Blossom Temple for six years, during which time the membership of the congregation nearly doubled. Many members embraced the new programs and recognized the importance of Project Isaiah, including the most revered member of all, the late Rabbi Gunther Plaut, may he rest in peace, and the president, Mrs. Henrietta Chesney.

Among the many new programs I organized, I also tailored youth and adult clubs to meet the specific needs of the Russian immigrant population who had been arriving in large numbers since the 1970s. One Erev Yom Kippur, I organized a supper in my little bungalow for about twenty new arrivals from the Soviet Union and Romania. None of them had ever set foot in a synagogue before, but were willing to try it out once I had obtained free tickets for them. During supper, I introduced them to the special meaning of the holiday, including why Jews fasted and details about the holiday prayers. Then we walked to the synagogue. By the time the service was well underway, I was completely enjoying it, feeling particularly proud of myself for having acquainted our new guests with a taste of Judaism. All of a sudden, the fire alarm interrupted and stopped the service, until the superintendent reassured us that it was a false alarm.

Two days later, I was summoned by the board of directors, who were quite agitated with what had transpired during the services with "my" Russians. Many of their members, clearly insensitive to the difficult task of familiarizing the Russians with our culture, had complained to the board about the immigrants. First of all, it turned out that two of their kids had triggered the fire alarm while running around in the hallway during the service. There was no excuse for that, they said. Was it realistic, I wondered, to expect that our norm of constraint be the same for this newly arrived group from the Soviet Union? Second, they scolded, none of "my" Russians even opened a prayer book. Had they considered that these Russians would have no interest in a book that had only Hebrew and English text in it, when they couldn't read a word of it? The third complaint was that "my" Russians were drinking water from the water fountain in the hall when they should have been fasting. Well, I took full responsibility for that – with all that I had to do, I had forgotten to explain to them that besides not eating, they weren't allowed to drink when fasting. My mistake, not theirs. Perhaps the first step of the project should have been to train the members of the board of directors on how to be a *mensch* when welcoming guests who had just left a country where Judaism had been suppressed and who were totally unfamiliar with synagogue behaviour.

～

Now that I had proved to myself that I was capable of working and raising my child, my dream was to enlarge the house. In 1981, I decided to extend the house in the back and build a second floor. Little did I know that I would have to build it pretty much step-by-step on my own. This required motivation, discipline, perseverance, integrity and courage. I learned what hard work and daily ritual can look like, and came to love our house dearly. At times, bashing down those walls was the best therapy for me in dealing with my anger. Our house became our home, representing stability and a haven for me and Romy. I was hoping that, in time, my parents would return to Canada and live with us.

Despite my efforts to save aggressively, costs were higher than I had anticipated. After the carpenters completed the foundation and the frame, and the electricity and plumbing was installed, I ran out of money and had to become my own contractor and construction worker. Of all of the workers, I must say I became the most reliable and steadiest. There were days when working full-time as a contractor/construction worker and running a private counselling practice from my home was so tiring that my head literally fell into my bowl of soup from exhaustion. While the construction work was physically demanding, counselling under these circumstances was mentally and emotionally challenging.

I practically lived at building stores and hardware stores, sourcing any knowledge I could muster out of the extremely helpful salespeople. After I had insulated the walls between the studs, neighbours and friends helped me place the big boards of drywall before I nailed them down. Then I nailed on metal corners. Walls, doors and windows were primed and painted twice. I also re-did the interior, removing six layers of linoleum from the pinewood floors, sanding, staining and varnishing the floors, and stripping, priming and painting the doors, windows and frames.

Many a night Romy and I would sleep in the open, on the upper floor balcony, under the crown of our maple tree, because the walls were still too wet and the fumes too toxic to live in. Other times we slept in the finished basement. By the end of 1981, both the exterior and interior of the house were ready.

I invited my friends to a housewarming party. They had prepared a promissory note for me to sign, declaring that I would never again embark on such an exhausting and complicated undertaking. I signed the note but could not keep my promise. A few months later, I started working on my PhD in counselling psychology, which proved to be equally challenging.

⁓

After my parents left Canada to go back to Israel, my mother did not communicate with me for seven years and did not allow my father to do so either. I kept writing to them but never heard back. Even when my father passed away in 1981, I wasn't notified. My mother later explained to me that she didn't want me to come to the funeral because of the huge expense, which she knew I couldn't possibly afford, and because I had just started a new position at the Department of Employment and Immigration that she didn't want to jeopardize. She knew all this because we had been hearing about one another through Aunt Mila. After my father's death, my mother started writing to me. She was truly concerned about my financial situation, as was I. Two years after my father died, she came back to Toronto and lived with us for one year, but living together still proved to be impossible, so she moved to the Baycrest Terrace retirement centre. My mother was always emotionally closed, and when the social worker at Baycrest tried to get her to talk about her past experiences in Transnistria, my mother absolutely refused, saying, "If you want to know about the Holocaust, take a book from the library and read."

For several years Romy and I, like my mother and I before us, had difficulties with each other. Mother-daughter relationships are often challenging, and ours was no different. Romy had a mind of her own and, of course, I had my own way of seeing things. I wanted her to pursue sciences at university because she was very good at it in high school and I wanted to be sure that she would have a steady career for life, but she loved singing and had her mind set on it. She registered at the Royal Conservatory of Music to pursue a musical career instead. I was torn by her choice because on the one hand I wanted her to be financially secure, and on the other, I knew that my daughter had a special gift: a voice like velvet, full and beautiful, as well as an insatiable passion for singing and acting. Romy felt that her opinion did not count; that she was not validated by me as a person in her own right; and that her individual needs and wishes were not being met. At nineteen, she moved out, and I felt a terrible loss.

After Romy left, she pursued her music, as she had wanted to. She became a singer, actor, producer, director, teacher, holistic therapeutic-voice specialist, and a broad-based activist for social justice. I am most proud of who she is and what she has accomplished in her life. Romy married a soft-spoken, jovial man, Richard. He was a computer specialist and later, when he retired, he started to produce a variety of art projects. Richard is a marvellous storyteller and has a great sense of humour. I am glad to say that they have been together for many years now and love each other dearly.

In the 1990s, with my permission, one of my patients in Toronto passed on my name and contact information to her husband's co-worker, Bill, "a nice man who was a recent widower." We met only a few months after his wife of thirty years had passed away. Bill and his wife had emigrated from Scotland with their two boys, Martin Brien and Erik Marcel, and their third, William Arthur, was born in Canada. They came temporarily, in search of a better life, and after five years decided to stay.

Bill called me up and we went out for coffee. Neither of us was particularly impressed by the other on that first date. He was very laid-back and far too introverted. I felt like I had to carry the entire conversation, with him saying only a few words. The few times that he did manage to speak up, he spoke in this heavy Scottish accent that was difficult for me to understand. I, in turn, came across to him like a ton of bricks: too loud and far too outspoken. There seemed to be a silent agreement between us: we knew that we were far too different to be involved in a relationship, and it was best that we not meet again. I was used to European men who would try to impress a woman with their charm, flirtation, humour or simply by showing off. Bill did not possess any of these attributes. And so, it was far from love at first sight for both of us. But a few weeks later I had to move a couch in the house and needed another pair of hands. Since none of my friends were available, I decided to call Bill. He came and helped me without reservation, which I liked. I was grateful for his help and made him dinner. We had a pleasant enough time. He came back another day – why not? We started exchanging our life stories, and slowly a relationship started to develop.

Romy and Bill immediately got along splendidly and, to my surprise, so did my mother and Bill. My mother had never liked anybody I dated, but she was delighted with Bill. It is true that she would have preferred that I marry a nice, rich doctor or lawyer, but she eventually compromised with Bill being an engineer. Romy used to say to me, "You had to reach the age of sixty to bring home a guy your mother liked." In fact, my mother felt so close to Bill that when she was in a coma for a few days before she passed away, she held on to Bill's hand much more than to mine.

Bill had an amazingly calming effect on me. Rather than flying off the handle, which was my typical reaction when I became angry, I could work through things with him. Feeling more stable emotionally allowed me to also work on my relationship with Romy. It was not an easy process, as I needed to hear just how much pain I had caused her over the years, which made me feel terribly guilty. It was worth the effort, though, because at the end of it Romy and I became closer. We were able to be together, go out together and openly express our love for each other. She is a very important part of my life and now I am able to treat her more respectfully, like the adult she is.

The first few years of my relationship with Bill were very difficult for both of us, but I began to appreciate Bill's qualities more and more. He was gentle, kind, loyal and sincere, just like my father. People often tell me that – that I chose a mate who is just like my father. My father was such a good man that he would literally give the shirt off his back to somebody in need. If someone forgot something in his store he would put a note in the window so when they came back to town, they could come and pick it up. Bill is that kind of a man: softspoken, polite, gentle, full of integrity.

I found that Bill's calm temperament gave me the freedom to follow my own pursuits, whether education, travel or writing a book. Most men would have tried to interfere when I wanted to take risks, but Bill didn't hold me back; in truth, he was holding me together. If I jumped into my "projects" too quickly and was not realistic, Bill pulled me back only to prop me back up. When I was plagued by nightmares and Bill became the target of my fists, knees and short but sharp fingernails, he gently restrained me until I regained composure. Bill accepted my insatiably strong creative spirit and never felt threatened by it. All in all, I can honestly say that Bill and I love each other dearly and we are embracing the last chapter of our lives together gracefully.

~

In 1992, Bill and I decided to visit Israel, which is so dear to my heart. We included a stop in Turkey, since it is close by and both of us were interested in the country. It was Bill's first visit to both countries. In Israel, we stayed with my aunt Sidi in Kiryat Bialik. We travelled by bus to the cities of Akko, Nahariya and Haifa, where we were mesmerized by the juxtaposition of biblical sights and ultramodern ones. We continued on by train to Tel Aviv to catch a bus tour to Jerusalem. En route to Jerusalem the tour stopped at Beit Lechem, or Bethlehem, Masada and the Dead Sea. We visited the biblical tombs of Rachel and Joseph, then drove up to Jerusalem, visiting the famous Kotel, the Western Wall. I was surprised by Bill's emotional reaction to the Kotel. From Jerusalem we travelled north to Nazareth, the Sea of Galilee and many other small towns.

Returning to Israel for the first time since 1962, I was struck by the many changes from the time I had lived there. The country was much more built up, the architecture charming and varied. Bill and I were delighted when we realized that every taxi driver could easily engage in a scholarly conversation about the Bible and had a clear point of view when it came to politics in Israel. What affected us most was the special kind of energy we felt from people, especially in Jerusalem. We couldn't help but be excited about everything we saw and everyone we spoke to.

Then we took a short plane ride to Istanbul, Turkey. We visited the city and the Grand Bazaar. People were extremely friendly and hospitable, extending invitations to come to their homes wherever we went. We visited many museums and the former palaces of several sultans. After Istanbul our bus tour took us to Gallipoli, Çanakkale, Troy, Izmir and Ephesus. In Ephesus we ate at a restaurant that advertised "fried lady's thighs," a funny but poor English translation of chicken thighs. From there we drove to Antalya, Konya and Ankara, where we saw all kind of memorials to Atatürk, the first president of Turkey, who abolished the Arabic alphabet and established a democratic republic. It was an extremely educational trip and we learned to appreciate Turkish history, culture and many ancient ruins.

In 1993, Bill and I flew to Scotland to visit his two brothers and their families. We stayed at the home of his older brother, Sam, and his wife, Betty. At the beginning of our trip Sam drove us through the southern part of the country; towards the end, Bill's younger brother, Colin, drove us through northern Scotland. The sights are very different from Canada; everything reminds you of antiquity and history. Scotland is quite charming, except for the rain every ten minutes.

Bill and I decided to do the last stretch of our travels in Scotland on our own. We joined a bus tour in Edinburgh, the capital city, and Glasgow, Scotland's largest city. In Edinburgh, we saw the Edinburgh Castle and other historic sites. In Glasgow, we made it a point to stop at the Giffnock and Newlands Hebrew Congregation, the largest shul in Scotland, and the Scottish Jewish Archive Centre, located in the Garnethill Synagogue. We rang the bell at the entrance and identified ourselves but were not allowed in until a security officer came down and did a full body search, even asking us to take off our shoes. After we were cleared, we were escorted to the centre, where we were surprised to see offices bustling with activity, given that there were only three thousand Jews living in Glasgow at that time.

Among the people we met in Glasgow was a woman in her sixties who lived on a farm and came there three times a week to study Jewish history and holidays. She had been brought up on a farm as a non-Jew. Her father died when she was in her fifties and her mother died when she was in her sixties, after revealing to her that she was in fact Jewish and had been adopted as a little girl from the pool of Kinder-transport children, the Jewish children who had been sent from Germany in 1938 and 1939 to England and Scotland by their parents to protect them from Nazi slaughter. Apparently there were not enough Jewish families in Scotland to adopt all of the children, so some were offered to gentiles. Her "mother" and "father" had adopted her because they were childless but raised her as if she had been their own daughter. What a shock it must have been to find out at the age of sixty that she was not who she thought she was all of her life!

~

When my mother passed away in 1995, the inheritance she left allowed us to purchase a timeshare in beautiful Puerto Vallarta, Mexico, which became our annual two-week reprieve from the Canadian snow and frost. One of the first things that struck us about Mexico was the sight of the Star of David in so many different contexts. It was not uncommon, for example, to see Mexican women adorned with Star of David earrings, necklaces or bracelets. In areas that tourists are not encouraged to visit, we also noticed the Star of David in metal railings, carved on wooden doors, and sometimes even on the pavement stones on these old streets. Intrigued, we asked locals why the Star of David was so prevalent and were told that it is a sign of good luck in financial affairs.

On one of our vacations there we were joined by a couple of dear friends, Erika and Steve Erdos, may his memory be blessed. One day the four of us ventured out to the surrounding hills. As we ascended, we noticed in the distance a large fresco on glass with the symbol of the tree of life. As we got closer we made out a Torah scroll, a *shofar* and a white dove. Driven by curiosity we ascended higher up the hill, until we reached a beautiful building with a huge tower that we climbed. At the top of the tower, there was a spectacular view of Banderas Bay. The entire façade of the building was made of beautiful stained glass with motifs.

Entering the building, we found a big hall that appeared to be a synagogue, with benches arranged around a bimah. On both sides of the bimah stood two large red armchairs, one with the name of Solomon, and the other with David inscribed on it. Behind the bimah was a deep basin that looked like a mikvah in white-and-blue mosaic. As we stood there in the hall, we heard the voices of a female choir rehearsing from another room. Interestingly, we later found out that this was a church, not a synagogue at all.

A few years later, we took a cruise that stopped in Guatemala. We were struck by the overwhelming beauty of the environment. The landscapes were breathtaking, with volcanic mountains, one of which was spewing smoke as we drove by. I remember visiting a macadamia-nut nursery, which was interesting since I knew nothing about how one of my favourite nuts grew. But our real fascination for this area only presented itself after our return to Toronto, when we discovered that among the predominately Christian population of Guatemala, there is a small group of about one hundred who, while searching for meaning in other religions, decided that Judaism would satisfy most of their needs.

In talking with friends about our Guatemalan trip, we subsequently learned that our long-time good friends, Amy Block and Paul Gelman, as well as Rabbi Elyse Goldstein, had been to Guatemala several times in the previous few years to help this small community with conversions, the study of Torah, bar mitzvahs and Jewish baby-naming celebrations. On each of their trips they brought boxes full of *kippot* (skullcaps), *talleisim* (prayer shawls) and prayer books. Bill and I are very interested in exploring and helping that community and hope to join them on a trip in the near future.

Shattered! 50 Years of Silence

Between the ages of ten and twelve, I knew only what was happening in my own shack in Shargorod. I found out about the history of Transnistria only when I did research for my book, starting in 1994. For a Holocaust survivor, writing about the Holocaust is a very difficult thing to do, foremost because we survivors have become experts at hiding the trauma of our past. For the longest time, it was taboo for anyone in our family to even mention Transnistria. It was critical that we did this in order to go on with our lives, yet continuing on with life was not normal in any sense of the word. Internally we harboured ongoing chronic grief: we mourned the terrible loss of our loved ones who had perished – those we knew and those that we didn't even get to know. We grieved over the loss of the hopes and dreams of our youth and the years lost in the camps that we will never recover. We were in a constant state of angst, trying desperately to appear normal in spite of our deep scars.

When the approximately 50,000 surviving Jewish deportees returned to Romania in 1944, in the hope of finding relatives from whom they had been separated in the trains or on the marches, they found that Romania was now governed by many of the same people who had murdered Jews during the pogroms and deported us to Transnistria. The government had merely changed the country's flag and their party slogan. Therefore, talking about the tragedy in Trasnistria was officially taboo. And the thriving cultural and religious life, the network of vibrant Jewish institutions and the contributions of the Jewish community to the development of Romania, just vanished.

Even in Canada, we survivors were too traumatized to reveal our suffering and losses; and when we occasionally did, we found that nobody was interested. In fact, many people tried to diminish our tragedy by telling us that they "too had to stand in line to obtain some rationed meat or herring." Others accused us of cowardice because we did not take on the armed guards. When Transnistria survivors heard about the mass murders in the gas chambers in the death camps in Poland, they felt that the more conventional murders in Transnistria were comparatively "not so bad."

While the Allied forces in Europe documented and publicized their findings after they liberated the camps in Europe, the Soviet army, which liberated Transnistria, did not. On the contrary, the Soviets downplayed the fact that Jews were murdered in the territories that they freed. They did not consider Jews as a national identity, and referred to Jewish victims in Ukraine simply as "Soviet citizens" rather than acknowledging their separate Jewish identity. I found this quite upsetting. By clumping Jews together with Soviet citizens, commemoration turned into empathy for the Soviets at large rather than specifically for the innocent Jews who were the targets of the majority of the deliberate mass civilian killing during the war.

However, the Romanian administration went even further, absolving some Romanian government officials and the Romanian people of blame and instead blaming the Germans for imposing fascist policies on them, thereby virtually erasing the Romanian role in the Holocaust. There were few war crimes trials for Romanian perpetrators. For all of these reasons, I consider Transnistria as forgotten before it was remembered; forgotten along with it is the memory of the pogroms, which killed thousands, as well as the thousands of Jewish men who were taken as slave labourers to the Danube delta and to other back-breaking projects.

The estimated figures of both deportations to Transnistria and deaths that occurred in Romania during the war vary: between 150,000 and 170,000 Romanian Jews were deported to Transnistria; of that number, approximately 110,000 perished there. More than 25,000 Roma were deported to Transnistria as well, of whom about 11,000 died. In total, between 280,000 and 380,000 Romanian and Ukrainian Jews died in territories under Romanian administration, between 150,000 and 250,000 of them in Transnistria.

One of the most distressing aspects for a survivor is seeing the distortion of facts related to the Holocaust. Coping with our horrendous past is one thing, but discovering that it is then being whitewashed is another. Fabrication of history is the ultimate betrayal. I am obviously most sensitive to the historical distortions of the Holocaust in Romania and Transnistria, given that I survived the Holocaust in Romania only to be thrust into the communist post-Holocaust era.

So many professionals have tried to talk about or explain the Holocaust, but no matter how much they try to approach this difficult subject, it is not at all the same as "living it," as a survivor does. The survivor's point of view is unique and many of us have gone to great lengths to share our stories while we are still alive.

I become particularly frustrated when someone who has never lived through the Holocaust assumes that he or she knows how we survivors feel about it. In 1975, I read an infuriating article in a professional counselling magazine from the US, where the author stated that all Holocaust survivors suffer from "survivor's guilt," a belief that was quite common in the mental health field at that time. I wrote a rebuttal to the article, stating that as a survivor I had no sense of guilt whatsoever. I had never done anything immoral to survive: I didn't steal bread from anybody and I didn't cheat anybody – and even if a survivor needed to do these acts to survive, would the outcome have been guilt? I feel extremely saddened about the losses we experienced, but I don't feel guilty about them. Thank goodness that "survivor's guilt" is no longer a commonly held point of view. It did not help any of the survivors understand their feelings; on the contrary, it only burdened many of us with feelings we did not experience at all.

The inspiration for writing a book about Transnistria literally fell on the ground before me. In 1993, Bill bought a book about a factory in Transnistria that helped save the lives of thousands of people. Respecting my need to stay away from Holocaust literature so that I would not be retraumatized by it, Bill read the book and placed it on our bookshelf without mentioning it to me. One day, when I was dusting and rearranging our bookshelves, the book fell on the floor: *Jagendorf's Foundry* by Siegfried Jagendorf was the first book I saw in English about Transnistria. It was about a dilapidated factory in Mogilev where many Romanian deportees were saved from death because the factory required them as labourers for repairs and maintenance. Not only had engineers been selected for this job, but somehow other professionals such as doctors, dentists or lawyers pretended to be engineers in order to be selected. Reading about this had a powerful impact on me. I sat on the floor, leaning my back against the sofa, and read and cried for three days. This was so cathartic for me that I wrote an article about Transnistria for *The Canadian Jewish News*, which was published on June 23, 1994.

After the article was published, I received a flood of phone calls from Transnistria survivors from all over the world. Apparently survivors from Toronto had sent the article to friends and relatives in many other countries. Whether the call was from Canada, the US, Israel or Europe, the reaction was the same – everyone was thrilled to see Transnistria mentioned in print for the first time. It was 1994 and hardly anyone knew about our suffering and about those who perished there. With this kind of response, I knew I had to do something to change that.

In July 1994, I spearheaded a local Transnistria Survivors' Association. Three months later, we held our first event, the first commemoration in the world, to my knowledge, of Transnistria victims. We decided that the event should take place in October, since October 1941 was the month when most deportations took place in Romania. As the founder and elected president of the Transnistria Survivors' Association, I made a point of inviting leaders from the Jewish and general community who, surprisingly, knew nothing about Transnistria, despite many having taught Holocaust studies for forty-five years. After the commemoration, the association continued organizing various events, including trips to the Holocaust Memorial Museum in Washington, DC, and social events for survivors. The goal was to ensure that we had a place to meet to remember our losses and honour our memories.

With so little awareness in the community about Transnistria, I wondered to what extent information was available on the subject. Bill and I began researching in libraries only to discover that, in stark contrast to other areas of Holocaust studies, where there was a wealth of information, with the exception of a couple of mentions in reference books or a few testimonials written in languages other than English – inaccessible to the general public – there were hardly any English-language books about Transnistria. Although about thirty years ago, twelve volumes of Jean Ancel's *Documents Concerning the Fate of Romanian Jewry during the Holocaust* had been published, it was first available only in Romanian, and the English translation was difficult to find. I decided then and there to make it my personal mission to publish a comprehensive book on Transnistria, in English, to fill the existing gap in Holocaust literature. I had the uncanny feeling that the writing of this book to bear witness and expose the horrors of Transnistria to the world at large was my life's meaning and the purpose of my survival.

Taking on this massive undertaking became an obsession. Recognizing that the survivors were aging and would soon no longer be alive to share their stories, I fought time. I was sixty-three and worked on this project with all my heart and soul. How ironic that, as a psychologist, here I was working towards this goal with such urgency and obsessiveness. I was in a constant state of anxiety and driven by an irrational fear that a truck might hit me before I completed the work!

I was not an author, and certainly not a historian. Who was I to undertake such an important historical work? I did not have the slightest idea how to start this project, but I was determined to do it. Throughout my entire professional career, I had never had to do any typing because my secretaries always had, and I knew there would be a massive amount of typing, which was a daunting thought. As far as my English was concerned, I knew I was lacking in the level of proficiency needed for this undertaking. Even though I had a PhD, my spelling was atrocious, and I was more familiar with academic rather than vernacular English, which I thought this type of book would require.

After considerable thought, I've decided to include in this memoir something I have never shared publicly because I was always afraid of being negatively labelled. My intention in writing about this is to dispel similar fears for my readers. I consider myself as someone who has two anomalies, both of which I have been acutely aware of in the past thirty years. The word anomaly has two definitions: a deviation from or departure from the normal; and a person who is peculiar, irregular or difficult to classify.

Firstly, I have dyslexia, a learning disorder which means that reading can be a challenge. Needless to say, this created many difficulties in my extensive academic work, as well in researching and compiling my anthology. These difficulties were compounded by the fact that English is not my mother tongue and I never took any formal lessons in the language.

Secondly, I have synesthesia, a condition that affects the perception of sense. I perceive vowels in colour – for instance, I see the letter "a" as white, the letter "u" as black and so on, which means that I can see the words "banana, Alabama, Tamara, Amanda, Atlanta, Alaska" as all white, even though they mean entirely different things. This anomaly was simultaneously helpful and confusing in my acquiring fluency in seven languages and getting by with another four. I think it was my synesthesia in action that caused some of the amusing incidents I mentioned when learning both Hebrew and English. It is my hope that people who have such anomalies will not suffer from low self-esteem, or let them interfere with what they wish to accomplish in life.

I had already toyed with the idea of early retirement, and the book was the final incentive to do it. In 1995 I gave up my secure job of fourteen years as a staff counsellor with the federal government, as well as my private practice in counselling, to focus my full-time attention on this book. Instead of going on vacation with Bill, as we had planned, I felt the money would be better spent on acquiring a computer for the project. Bill said, "What do you need a computer for? You are computer illiterate!" "Yes," I said, "but I have to write a book." That was all I needed to say to get Bill on board. We went to several computer stores to purchase a computer. When I saw three- and four-year olds running their little fingers across the keyboards I said to myself, "If they can do it, I can learn how to do that, too."

My drive pushed me forward. Convinced that I had no time to spare or to take any computer training, I stumbled my way through word processing by using trial and error. Bill and Romy assisted with the research, while I sat there fully immersed, typing with two fingers, until finally my Swedish friend, Siv Linnea Petterson, came to the rescue. She moved in with us for about nine months and was extremely helpful in teaching me computer skills and helping me write the text. Since we were glued to the computer all day long, Bill had no choice other than to take on the household chores, which he did willingly, in addition to his full-time employment.

Initially, I had planned to produce a book of between one hundred and fifty and two hundred pages, just so that there would be something published about the history of Transnistria in the English language. However, it appeared that God had a different plan. Mysteriously, word got out that I was working on this book, and I re-

ceived dozens of documents, historical resources and personal testimonies from Transnistria survivors worldwide. I selected about fifty
important government documents for the book, some of which were
stamped "secret and urgent." Siv and I proceeded to translate them
from Romanian. Bill tried to help with the war lingo, but none of us
were familiar with Romanian war terminology. We did the best we
could.

The book took on a momentum of its own, totally controlling
my life. I felt as if a guiding force was standing behind my computer chair, directing relevant material to me and infusing me with a
stream of energy, persistence and faith. Doubt, frustration and
impatience were present as well. The latter is one of my biggest
shortcomings. It became clear that I was not the only one who was
impatiently waiting for me to complete this book. Shortly after I began the initial research stage of the work, I began receiving phone
calls from people asking how soon the book would be ready. Their
impatience came from their need to get a copy to one of their dying
relatives who might benefit from seeing such a book in print before
they passed away. However, this wasn't simply a matter of pressing a
few buttons on a keypad. It took close to one year of self-imposed focus to finish the first draft of the book. We edited and corrected that
draft seven times, an enormously draining task for just two people
who were unfamiliar with what had to be done next.

The draft version consisted of more than five hundred pages; the
first two hundred pages described the geopolitical history of Transnistria, with maps and official documents, and the final three hundred pages contained personal testimonies of survivors in Canada,
Israel, Romania, Russia and Venezuela. I had to translate and edit
material from Romanian, Russian, Hebrew, Spanish and Yiddish.
Every testimony drew me into the suffering of its author, which emotionally exhausted me because I identified with each survivor's story
as if it were my own. I became overly concerned that the work be finished, lest the English record of the Transnistria tragedy remain un-

published. Nothing in my life mattered at that point but the completion of the project. At every stage of the work, I distributed copies of my disks to friends, just in case something should happen to me.

When the manuscript was edited and proofread, I thought that our work was finished. How terribly wrong I was! Not having any previous experience with book publishing, I had no idea that finding a publisher, a printer, a graphic artist and a bookbinder would be so demanding. By that time I was on the verge of a nervous breakdown, but once again, I was guided by a strong invisible force. What an incredible learning experience it was. However, I was not yet at the end of my trials and tribulations.

Several days after the graphic artist delivered the proofs to the printer, I experienced another "divine" intervention. A gentleman from Toronto by the name of Sorin Finkelstein phoned, looking for information on Transnistria. He told me that he had lost most of his family in Transnistria and asked if I could help him with his son's high school project on this subject. I invited him to my home and showed him the edited draft of the book. As he read our translation of the Romanian documents, I noticed an expression of disapproval on his face. It turned out that all of the translations pertaining to the war lingo, such as the ranks of officers, military equipment and Romanian government decrees, were totally incorrect. I felt crushed. Trying to console me, Sorin volunteered to make the necessary corrections. The problem was that he could only work from 5:00 p.m. until 5:00 a.m.

The next crisis came when the graphic artist had a fire at her house, bringing the project to a halt for two more weeks. I had already called the printer twice with delays, so this postponement was not well received. Sorin and I continued to press on, working every night from 5:00 p.m. to 5:00 a.m. Bill was as supportive as usual but from time to time, I would hear him mumbling under his breath, "If Transnistria did not kill you fifty-five years ago, it is killing you now!" Regardless of the effort required, I knew that the accuracy of the translated documents was crucial. Even after the corrections were made, another round of editing and formatting had to be done. Paying for the professionals involved in this anthology required fundraising, and unfortunately none of the members of the Transnistria Association I founded were willing to contribute. I was beside myself. To ease the pressure, Bill and I decided to dip into our personal savings from our Retirement Savings Plans.

Finally, in 1997, a 536-page book titled *Shattered! 50 Years of Silence: History and Voices of the Tragedy in Romania and Transnistria* was published. It is the only English-language anthology on Transnistria that exists for the general public. As soon as the book was published, I sent a copy to the president of Romania, Mr. Emil Constantinescu. He gave a speech acknowledging the Holocaust in Romania on May 4, 1997, and I believe that this is why the Consul General of Romania from Toronto and the Secretary of the Romanian Embassy from Ottawa attended my book launch on May 15, 1997.

In the first year after publication, the book was honoured with two prestigious awards – the Canadian Society for Yad Vashem award for Holocaust History and Israel's Ianculovici Cultural Foundation award for Holocaust literature – and the demand for the anthology was higher than we had anticipated. I donated dozens of volumes of the book to libraries all over the world, and book orders came from as far away as Hawaii, Japan and Australia, not to mention Canada, the US, Israel and Europe. I received many letters of thanks from readers. At least three people discovered relatives they thought had died, and for others, the book gave them information on what had happened to their relatives. Some survivors mentioned in the book were even able to receive restitution money from the German government after the book's publication. These unexpected effects were very emotional and rewarding for me. In one funny incident, a gentleman called me from Germany and said that he had bought my book on Amazon, which was then sent to him from New Zealand. He was going to New

York for business and wanted to come to Toronto to have me sign the book. I felt flattered and agreed. When I opened the cover of the book to sign it, I was stunned to see the stamp of the Toronto Public Library. How did the book I had donated in Toronto end up in the hands of a man from Germany, who got it from New Zealand? Was this meant to be?

I am not a historian or professional writer. When I embarked on this project, I had no resources and was computer illiterate. I know, in the depth of my heart, that I could not have brought this book to light without the continuous guidance from an invisible force that I was privileged to experience during my work. Throughout the entire project, I felt that universal power guiding and supporting me every step of the way. I am very grateful for that. I now see the difficulties I encountered on this project as tests that I had to learn to overcome.

Since my English became better, I continued to write, and I had articles published in presses in Toronto, the US, Israel and Romania. I am also a thirty-year contributing lecturer at the Holocaust Education Centre in Toronto.

The Visual History of the Shoah

In 1993, as result of the movie *Schindler's List*, a lot of survivors wrote to Steven Spielberg and travelled to see him to ask that their story be told. In response, Spielberg set up the Survivors of the Shoah Visual History Foundation in Los Angeles. The goal of the foundation was to capture the stories of Holocaust survivors. Over the course of five years, survivors living in about one hundred countries were interviewed in seventy different languages, and local people were trained to do the interviewing. After interviewing the survivors, the Foundation interviewed Righteous Gentiles as well. The whole project is now digitized in such a way that if you type in my place of birth, date of birth, and name – say, Dorna, Felicia Steigman-Carmelly, September 25, 1931 – the interview should come up.

Even though most people who applied to become interviewers were not survivors, I applied and was accepted. Some interviewers conducted only one interview a week because of the emotionally exhausting nature of dealing with the horrors, but I completed three interviews a week because I could handle what I was already familiar with. I interviewed survivors who were living in Toronto and in other cities in Ontario. During these interviews I discovered that unless they had relatives in Transnistria, were survivors of Transnistria themselves, or were from areas such as Bessarabia and Bukovina, most of the interviewees, even if they were Romanian, had never heard of Transnistria.

In the spring of 1995, I was recruited to interview in St. Petersburg because I could speak Russian. Getting the necessary travel documents was a complicated and lengthy process because the Foundation had to receive an invitation for the interviewers from somebody in Russia. While the Foundation was arranging for my documents, my mother had a stroke and passed away; may she rest in peace. I had to leave for Russia the day after my mother's shiva was over. That was extremely difficult, but I decided to go anyway. I knew that I was irreplaceable, given the lengthy time it would have taken to get the documents for somebody else.

The trip to St. Petersburg took about twenty-five hours. A huge national war veterans' convention was going on there at that time. The Foundation decided to take advantage of all of the interviewees being in one place rather than have us travel from place to place across Russia. We were organized into teams of interviewers, assistants and videographers. The interview scheduling was gruelling. We were to conduct three interviews a day to ensure that we could maximize the number of veterans interviewed before the end of the convention. The convention was held at the large, lovely Hotel Moskva, where the convention attendees as well as the interview teams were lodged. Many of these men had been in the Soviet army and others, not in the official army for one reason or another, had been in the underground resistance.

We didn't anticipate the length of time it would take to get the background details of each interviewee. In Ontario it took only five minutes to get someone's name, date of birth and place of birth. Here, it could take an hour or more! This was because after World War II, the Soviet regime was extremely suspicious of anyone who was not in the military – such as partisans and POWs – and considered such people potential traitors. Consequently, many non-military men did their utmost to change their identity and fled to the most remote places in the country. Wherever they went they used bribery to obtain new identification papers, with a new name, date of birth and place of birth. Upon arrival in a new location, if the men saw anyone who looked at all familiar, they feared they might be recognized and so moved on, again accessing new identity papers. And so, when it came to interviewing these men, every time they told us their personal information, there was inevitably earlier personal information that we needed to uncover for accuracy. This situation slowed our demanding interview process to a snail's pace.

I was in St. Petersburg on the last day of Pesach, and I had made earlier arrangements, from Toronto, to take half a day off then to go to a synagogue to say Kaddish for my mother. Well, little did I know that I would be picked up by a car driven by an official bodyguard, who took me to a synagogue and stayed with me as long as I needed to say Kaddish. I wasn't sure if the bodyguard was supposed to protect me from the Russians or vice versa.

The synagogue was built in 1904 and had not been used from 1918 until 1990, so it was pretty run down. I could see some remnants of its former glory: the gorgeous, full-crystal chandeliers now covered in spider webs; the white- and grey-veined marble columns with cracks running through them; beautiful stained-glass windows, now caked in mud; and the floor and benches, whose boards had rotted from the passage of time. Downstairs in the men's section there were about twenty-five men praying, while upstairs about fifteen women were bent over books. My bodyguard followed closely behind me as I went to the upstairs section. Though shabbily dressed in worn-out sweaters or shirts, both men and women wore dozens of war medals on their chests. Since there had not been any Jewish education in the country for close to seventy years, none of the women and few of the men knew how to read a Hebrew prayer book. Even so, a young lady sitting in front of me kept looking into a book. This sparked my curiosity and I bent over to see what it was. It was a Russian Haggadah, the Jewish text for Passover, not usually meant for religious services. I spoke to a few people about it and they gave me one as a souvenir of the occasion. I still treasure it. They told me that it had been distributed by the American Jewish Joint Distribution Committee just before Passover.

In total, from my hours volunteering in both Ontario and Russia, I interviewed close to two hundred Holocaust and war survivors. During the interviews I realized that most Holocaust survivors, like me, had suppressed their wartime experiences. For many of us, the wounds were so raw and so deep that it took us forty or fifty years to even begin talking about them. Yet, throughout our lives, the most insignificant as well as the most important events we encountered were always superimposed against the backdrop of the trauma of the camps. All survivors of the Nazi/Fascist camps suffered and continue to suffer from nightmares and a myriad of other psychological problems. These historical events may be part of the past, but the Holocaust will remain alive as long as we are.

Journeys

I am extremely fortunate to have travelled quite extensively throughout my life. Travel gave me the chance to get to know cultures and traditions different from my own, which broadened my awareness of who I am and how I fit as a Jew within the world at large. As I was writing my memoir, I realized just how much all of the people who have crossed my path – family, friends, clients and coworkers – have been intertwined with my travels.

One was my old friend Eva, with whom I had shared an apartment in Bucharest after the war. She eventually settled in Curaçao, an island in the Caribbean that is a constituent of the Netherlands. For three consecutive summers, she invited me to travel with her to the surrounding islands of Aruba, Bonaire and Saint Martin. All three islands had Jewish inhabitants, whose descendants had immigrated after the Spanish Inquisition and had built synagogues in which to gather and pray.

In Curaçao I visited the Mikvé Israel-Emanuel Synagogue, one of the oldest synagogues in the Americas. The synagogue has floors covered with sand; explanations for sand floors vary, but one is that it replicates the actions of Jews who had been forced to convert to Catholicism during the Spanish Inquisition but secretly continued to practise Judaism – the sand floors muffled the sound of their shoes and prayers. Next to the synagogue is the Beit Chaim Bleinheim cemetery, one of the oldest Jewish cemeteries still in use in the Western world.

Another of my trips was to Belgium to visit my old friend Peter from Bucharest, his wife, Ana-Marie, and their son, Radu. Peter had written to me during the time I lived in Montreal. He told me that Ana-Marie had managed to defect from Romania to Belgium when she had been given permission to travel there for a convention, but Peter and five-year-old Radu were left behind in Bucharest. Ana-Marie had also written me then, informing me of her plans to seek asylum in Belgium and her hope that the International Red Cross would be able to help Peter and Radu obtain permission to join her. I sent money and parcels of clothing and shoes to Ana-Marie and continued corresponding with both her and Peter. She eventually settled down in a small town called Mouscron, but it wasn't until eleven years later that Peter and Radu managed to join her.

When I visited them, we travelled to Antwerp and Bruges in Belgium, and Amsterdam and Made in the Netherlands. Although we saw many famous and interesting museums, it was the reunion with Peter and his family that was most exciting for me. When Peter later came to visit me, I tried to reciprocate their hospitality with a road trip to Niagara Falls, Montreal and Quebec City. To this day, we still remain in touch.

I also travelled to Sweden with Romy and my good friend Siv, who helped me write my book, *Shattered*. We flew to Stockholm and stayed with Siv's hospitable relatives, continued by train and ferry to Oslo, the capital of Norway, and then to the city of Bergen. In Bergen, we visited the house of Norway's most famous composer, Grieg, which is now a museum. Since Grieg's wife had not allowed him to compose in the house because "the noise disturbed her," he had a little cabin built down the hill by the river where he composed his music. At his grave, the three of us, separately, had an unworldly experience. As we stood there, we felt the air around us become freezing cold and sensed Grieg playing music for us. It was really eerie when we shared this experience with one another.

Two of my most exotic and interesting trips came about when my cousin from South Carolina, Dr. Murray Treiser, a plastic surgeon, invited me to join him on his travels. Murray is also an academic, a writer and a teacher of Kabbalah, Jewish mysticism, at the Jewish Studies Center in the College of Charleston, South Carolina. Murray insisted, to my delight, that wherever we travelled, the main purpose would be to visit Jewish institutions and the offices of Chabad Lubavitch, an Orthodox Jewish organization impressive for its anti-poverty work and for its preservation of Jewish infrastructure worldwide. Both Murray and I were excited by this adventure of going to learn about life in faraway places and getting a chance to meet the locals.

Our first major adventure was to India, Nepal and Bhutan in December 2000. Murray had meticulously planned everything, including car, driver and private guide for each location. We met up in the airport in Frankfurt and flew to New Delhi, where we continued on by car and plane through a large area called Rajasthan.

India has a totally different way of life from ours here in North America. While people here are always on the run for one thing or another, the pace of life in India is much, much slower, although you would never know it if you looked at the traffic or marketplace. The roads are jammed with everything from transport and funeral trucks and rickshaws to cows, which are a sacred animal in India, baboons, geese and goats. In the market, in the midst of the hustle and bustle of people selling just about everything, stands a dentist pulling teeth, a barber trimming hair and beards, or a shoemaker fixing shoes. At times I truly felt like we were on a different planet.

The places that I will forever remember are the Taj Mahal, Varanasi, the holiest of the seven sacred cities in Hinduism and Jainism, and the Khajuraho Group of Monuments, a complex of Hindu and Jain temples that have wall carvings depicting the everyday life of the common people of India – potters, farmers and other folk. We were surprised to see, at the entrance of such a grand historic site, a small kiosk where an Israeli vendor was selling hummus and falafel. Although it seemed so out of context for us, for this vendor it was home, at least for now.

We visited several synagogues in India, some of them Ashkenazi and others Sephardi, as well as Chabad Lubavitch offices. We were impressed by the activities of Chabad. Murray left large donations in each one of these institutions and, as a result, received many blessings in gratitude for his generosity.

We also had the opportunity to visit Jewish families who had been living in India for many generations. The older generation seemed content to live out the rest of their lives in India, whereas the younger generation was making, or already had, plans to immigrate to Israel or North America for what they perceived to be a more prosperous life.

Bhutan, a tiny, remote and impoverished kingdom nestled in the Himalayas between its powerful neighbours, India and China, was next on our travel list. Bhutan's ancient Buddhist culture and breathtaking scenery make it a natural tourist attraction. However, tourism is restricted; visitors must travel as part of a pre-arranged package or guided tour.

The Bhutanese monarchy has a philosophy called Gross National Happiness, which strives to achieve a balance between the spiritual and the material. Everyone must wear the national dress, for men a knee-length wrap-around tailored from patterned material and for women a white blouse and jumper-like gown of different colours and designs. I was intrigued that there were still places in our world where one has to obey a certain code of dress, but then I remembered the Hasidic men right here in Toronto, who wear the garb of ancient rabbis in their honour.

From Bhutan we took a short plane ride to Nepal over the range of the ten tallest mountains in the world, including Mount Everest.

Behind us sat a man and a woman, whom we overheard talking about visiting the Lubavitch Rabbi in Kathmandu, Nepal's capital and largest metropolis. I poked Murray with my elbow, knowing that such a plan was impossible given the lack of Jews in this area, where the majority of the population is Hindu and the minority Buddhist, Muslim and Christian.

To our great surprise, we discovered there was indeed a Lubavitch centre in Kathmandu. We later visited it and met the rabbi there, who was extremely friendly and very dedicated. After Murray and I left the centre, we were amused by a kosher salami that we saw hanging in the window of a nearby grocery store – a true sign that, though few in number, Jews did exist in this part of the world.

In May 2007, Murray and I took our second exotic trip across the world – an extensive tour of Central Asia, Bulgaria and Romania. We went first through the five "stans": Kazakhstan, Kyrgyzstan, Tajikistan, Uzbekistan and Turkmenistan.

In Kazakhstan there are eighteen synagogues, but we had time to visit only two, in addition to the Chabad Lubavitch Centre. We drove through Kyrgyzstan, a mountainous country with beautiful lakes that sparkled in the view from the mountains. Despite the impoverished conditions, the local folk were extremely friendly and did not hesitate to open their homes to us wherever we went. In Bishkek, Kyrgyzstan's capital, we saw some industry and large, older buildings, but none of the elegant, multi-storey apartment buildings we saw elsewhere in Central Asian cities. But seeing so many happy children running through the streets was a wonder to the eye and a delight to the heart. Despite Kyrgyzstan's large population, only a small number of Jews live there now; thousands immigrated to Israel in the decades following World War II.

After Kyrgyzstan we drove through Tajikistan, another mountainous country with a rapidly growing population. We were unable to contact any Jewish groups there because we were late in catching up with our pre-arranged tour for Uzbekistan. Uzbekistan was the most interesting of the "stans" for us, not because of its physical size or its large population, but because it had the largest Jewish community in all of Central Asia. Even so, Jews represented only one-third of 1 per cent of the population of twenty-seven million, which is mostly Uzbeks and other minorities, including Russians, Tajiks, Kazakhs and Tatars. Many big cities have Jewish quarters so that the communities can live around synagogues, Jewish schools, cemeteries and other communal institutions. Synagogues and general museums display old Jewish artifacts.

Some people say that the name Samarkand comes from the name Samaria in Israel. Is it possible that some of our ten lost tribes ended up in that area long ago? There are Ashkenazi and Sephardi communities in the country, but unfortunately there is quite a rift between them, and each community has its own institutions.

The first group of Ashkenazi Jews came to the region when Stalin sent Jews there as a form of punishment. Other Ashkenazi Jews joined this group when they fled Europe during the Holocaust. My aunt Sidi and the Kogans – my cousin Diana Treiser's in-laws – are examples of those who survived the war by making it to Uzbekistan. As I mentioned earlier, Sidi, who had lived in Beltz, Bessarabia, before the war, escaped by reaching Tashkent, where she spent the war years working in a fabric factory. The Kogans had lived in Kishinev, Bessarabia, before the war and, like Sidi, fled to Tashkent. My cousin Izi (Israel) Kogan was born in Tashkent. Many years later, my cousin Diana Treiser, the daughter of my aunt Mila and uncle Armin, married Dr. Israel Kogan.

The next part of our journey was a bus tour through Bulgaria with a group of tourists who all came from the United States. We began our tour in Sofia, the capital and largest city, situated at the foot of the Vitosha Mountain in the west of the country. Given its large Orthodox Christian majority, followed by a minority of Muslims and an even smaller grouping of Jews, we were surprised to find out that the Jewish high schools in Sofia drew many non-Jews. These schools, subsidized by American businessman and philanthropist Ronald Lauder, are among the very best in the country.

Other than Sofia, the city that made a particular impression on us was Plovdiv, situated in the south-central part of Bulgaria. Plovdiv, one of the oldest cities in the world, is the birthplace of Murray's younger son's wife, Raya. The six-thousand-year-old city is often referred to as the "City of the Seven Hills." While touring Plovdiv, we visited a very old synagogue with gorgeous Venetian glass chandeliers. Although the synagogue was beautiful, I couldn't help feeling a bit sad, knowing that this institution was one of the last remnants of a Jewish community that had long abandoned this metropolis for another.

On our tour we stopped at several commemorative sites that honoured Jews who had perished during the Holocaust. Bulgaria did not deport its own Jewish citizens during the Holocaust, but in 1943 it deported Jews living in the Greek and Yugoslav territories it had occupied two years earlier. They were not considered Bulgarian citizens, and most were killed at Treblinka.

From Bulgaria we crossed the Danube by ship to Romania, where I was hoping to see the Danube delta. I was keen to learn more about the history of the reconstruction of the Danube delta, where hundreds of Jewish men had been used as forced labourers and perished during World War II. Unfortunately, we didn't reach the delta, instead crossing the Danube where it was closest to Romania.

Our final destination was the country of my birth, Romania, which had betrayed my family during the war. Before World War II, Romania had a Jewish population of around 800,000, but thousands were murdered during the war. After the war, most of the Jewish survivors immigrated to Israel and North America, and at present there are only a few thousand left.

Our group visited what I would call the symbol of post-war Romania – the People's Palace in Bucharest, the largest civilian administrative building in the world, built during Ceauşescu's communist

regime to accommodate all of the ministries of the Romanian administration, as well as the chambers of the Romanian parliament. The
construction required the destruction of almost the entire historic
district, including churches, synagogues and thousands of small resi-
dences. This building is presently used as a museum. We ate dinner
at a restaurant in a famous park on a lake, where we saw a beautiful
performance of Romanian folk dances.

Driving through the country was a real treat; I enjoyed marvelling
at the landscape that somehow defied fascism and communism, having remained intact throughout the destruction of those oppressive
regimes. We saw the Bicaz Canyon, a natural passageway between
the Romanian provinces of Moldova and Transylvania dug out by
the waters of the Bicaz River. We continued on to nearby Bran Castle, often referred to by naive tourists as "Dracula's Castle," which it
is not. The historical figure that inspired Dracula, Vlad the Impaler,
was merely a guest at this well-preserved fortress from the Middle
Ages. The "real" Dracula Castle where Vlad resided is an out-of-the-
way ruin that does not attract many visitors because it is less dra-
matic. From there we proceeded on to Sinaia, a mountain resort; the
late nineteenth-century Peles Castle; a beautiful synagogue in Brașov,
where only a couple of hundred Jewish people remain; and, in the
province of Bukovina, the original Painted Monasteries, whose interior and exterior frescoes date back to the fifteenth and sixteenth
centuries.

Once we reached northeast Bukovina, we were not too far from
Dorna. Murray rented a car to drive us back to my hometown. I knew
roughly where my house was, but it took us a while to locate it. I remembered that it was on a one-block road off the main street, one
house before the train tracks and the Dorna River. We walked the
street many times before I recognized the house, which had been
white when we had lived there but was now black from layer upon
layer of grime. Gone was the beautiful house that I had remembered,
the consequence of years of neglect under communist rule, where

maintenance was a low priority. Even the cupola of the casino and the roofs of the therapeutic baths treatment buildings in town were rusty and dilapidated.

We searched for some Jewish people in Dorna, but there were none who had lived there before the war. There were a few elderly Jews from other areas, living in destitute conditions. The first thing that came to mind upon seeing the changes that had taken place over the years in Dorna was how relieved I was that my grandparents and my parents were not alive to witness them. It would have crushed their hearts.

Discouraged from seeing what had happened to our house and the buildings in town, we sought out what used to be our beautiful Temple, hoping that it remained intact. Instead what we found was one corner of the roof missing, the benches broken and the candelabras plundered. Once a holy sanctuary, the synagogue was now used as storage for old furniture.

Despairingly, we wandered towards the Jewish cemetery. We were told that a man living nearby had been hired to take care of it, only to discover that he had died and his wife had taken his place. After approaching the woman for help in entering the locked gate, she asked us for money to get in, with an angry look that suggested that we had violated her solitude. The site was so neglected and was in such disarray that we could not pass through the grounds because of the many fallen trees and fallen tombstones. We climbed over them in search of the graves of baby Pirika, Murray's sister who had died young, and my maternal grandmother, who had also been buried there. Some graves were merely large holes covered with grass so that when we tried to step over them, our feet sunk in and we felt as if the dead were pulling us in. There was no classification system whatsoever, so searching for these graves proved to be in vain. We were heartened when we unexpectedly came across some graves of our ancestors, the Rubingers.

As I stood by the graves, I reflected on all my adventures across the world and my return to Dorna, my birthplace and hometown. What stood before me were a black house, a plundered Temple and a neglected, decrepit cemetery – all symbols of the evil, painful world that had come out of and followed the Holocaust. Throughout my adult life I had thought that I would never be free from this world, feeling that although I had one foot in the present, my other foot was always stuck in that old world. But as I stood there with the warm wind on my face, I felt the ground shift. I knew that I had come full circle. I turned around to take one glance back and with both feet strongly planted on the ground, I left the cemetery, never to return.

Epilogue

Although writing this memoir has been emotionally difficult for me, it has also been one of the most liberating experiences I have undertaken in my life. Somehow it has validated my life's work and made me feel that my existence on this earth has meaning. This is extremely important at my age because the past becomes more and more important as the options for the future become more and more limited.

At some point in my writings, it dawned on me to what extent one stage of my life affected another, even if many years had transpired in between. I felt as though pieces of the puzzle had been given to me at different times, without any connection between them. Then, as I was writing this memoir, all the pieces fell into place and the puzzle was solved.

Although I was born into some privilege, it was stripped from me for being Jewish during the Holocaust. I also inherited the anxiety of my ancestors who had been persecuted long before the Holocaust. Despite this, I am proud to share one thing I have learned about life: to embrace life as a gift, despite the difficulties that come with it. If we shrink in the face of our difficulties, we will remain powerless and be defeated.

So if life is a gift, then what should we do with this gift? What exactly are we here on this earth to do? In my opinion, it is vital to be a good person. What I have learned from my life is that a good character depends on more than what we learn from our parents, where we are born, the degree of formal education we achieve, the religion we believe in, the size of our bank account or the type of work that we do.

It is true that to some extent good character comes from what we inherit from our past, but I truly believe that, by-and-large, good character is the result of our personal drive to overcome challenges. As such, I am forever grateful for all of the challenges that came my way. Although my life has been far from easy, it has certainly been vibrant and interesting.

The Jewish concept of *tikkun olam* has been a pillar in my life. As *tikkun olam* suggests, I believe that our purpose is to repair the world, making it a better place to live than how we found it. So if I helped anyone become even a little bit better because at some point I crossed his or her path, that makes me very happy. I also thank that person for crossing my path, for that person's life has most certainly enhanced mine.

I would like to conclude with all that I am most grateful for: Bill, for acting as my living dictionary; my family members, wherever they reside; my wonderful friends, who come from diverse religious backgrounds, for being a significant part of my life; the tiny piece of land called Israel, a place where I learned to breathe freely and love deeply; Canada, for providing me with a wonderful new home where I have been able to feel most secure; and last but not least, the spirit that has empowered and inspired me throughout my life.

Glossary

Allies The coalition of countries that fought against Germany, Italy and Japan (the Axis nations). At the beginning of World War II in September 1939, the coalition included France, Poland and Britain. Once Germany invaded the USSR in June 1941 and the United States entered the war following the bombing of Pearl Harbor by Japan on December 7, 1941, the main leaders of the Allied powers became Britain, the USSR and the United States. Other Allies included Canada, Australia, Czechoslovakia, Greece, Mexico, Brazil, South Africa and China. *See also* Axis.

American Jewish Joint Distribution Committee (JDC) Also known colloquially as the "Joint." A charitable organization founded in 1914 to provide humanitarian assistance and relief to Jews all over the world in times of crisis. It provided material support for persecuted Jews in Germany and other Nazi-occupied territories and facilitated their immigration to neutral countries such as Portugal, Turkey and China. Between 1939 and 1944, JDC officials helped close to 81,000 European Jews find asylum in various parts of the world. Between 1944 and 1947, the JDC assisted more than 100,000 refugees living in DP camps by offering retraining programs, cultural activities and financial assistance for emigration.

antisemitism Prejudice, discrimination, persecution and/or hatred against Jewish people, institutions, culture and symbols.

Antonescu, Marshal Ion (1882–1946) Prime minister of Romania from September 1940 to August 1944. Antonescu allied his country with Nazi Germany and under his dictatorial regime, anti-Jewish measures were implemented; more than 130 ghettos, and camps were established in Transnistria; and hundreds of thousands of Jewish civilians were killed. In 1946, he was executed for war crimes. *See also* Transnistria.

Ashkenazi (Hebrew) An adjective first used in the Middle Ages to describe Jews of Germanic descent; in the eleventh century, the term also came to encompass Jews of Central and Eastern European descent. *See also* Sephardic.

Atatürk, Mustafa Kemal (1881–1938) First president of Turkey. Atatürk established a secular, democratic republic in Turkey and brought in social and economic reforms.

Austro-Hungarian Empire Also known as the Dual Monarchy of Austria and Hungary, ruled by the royal Habsburg family. It was successor to the Austrian Empire (1804–1867) and functioned as a dual-union state in Central Europe from 1867 to 1918. A multinational empire, the Dual Monarchy was notable for the constant political and ethnic disputes among its eleven principal national groups. Although the Empire adopted a Law of Nationalities, which officially accorded language and cultural rights to various ethnic groups, in practice there were many inequalities in how the groups were treated. Jews were granted both citizenship rights and equal status to other minority groups but minorities such as the Slovaks were excluded from the political sphere, whereas Czechs were accepted into government positions. The Austro-Hungarian Empire dissolved at the end of World War I and divided into the separate and independent countries of Austria, Hungary and Czechoslovakia.

Axis The coalition of countries, including Germany, Italy and Japan, that fought against the Allies during World War II. The Axis powers formally signed an agreement of cooperation, the Tripartite

Pact, in September 1940. Other countries that joined the Axis included Hungary, Romania, Slovakia, Bulgaria, Yugoslavia and the Independent State of Croatia. *See also* Allies.

bimah (Hebrew) The raised platform in a synagogue from which the Torah is read.

British Broadcasting Corporation (BBC) The British public service broadcaster. During World War II, the BBC broadcast radio programming to Europe in German and the languages of the occupied countries. It was illegal to listen to these broadcasts, but many people in Nazi-occupied Europe turned to it as the most reliable source of news.

British Mandate Palestine The area of the Middle East under British rule from 1923 to 1948, as established by the League of Nations after World War I. During that time, the United Kingdom severely restricted Jewish immigration. The Mandate area encompassed present-day Israel, Jordan, the West Bank and the Gaza Strip.

Ceaușescu, Nicolae (1918–1989) Romanian Communist politician who served as general secretary of Romania's Communist Party (1965–1989) and as president from 1967 to 1989. His rule was marked by repression of rights such as free speech and economic export policies that caused the country's extreme shortages of food, medicine and other supplies. Ceaușescu was deposed in December 1989 following mass protests during what came to be known as the Romanian Revolution, and executed shortly thereafter.

Constantinescu, Emil (1939–) The president of Romania from 1996 to 2000.

Five-Year Economic Plan Based on Soviet models, Romania's set goals to develop its economy through government control of property, agriculture and production of goods and services. Beginning in 1951, Romania had a series of eight five-year plans, which ended with president Ceaușescu's fall in 1989. *See also* Ceaușescu, Nicolae.

gendarmes Members of a military or paramilitary force.

Hanoar Hatzioni (Hebrew) The Zionist Youth. A socialist-Zionist group that began in Europe in 1926 to educate youth in Jewish and Zionist principles and to encourage self-actualization through living in Israel. *See also* Zionism.

Hashomer Hatzair (Hebrew) The Youth Guard. A left-wing Zionist youth movement founded in Central Europe in the early twentieth century to prepare young Jews to become workers and farmers, to establish kibbutzim – collective settlements – in pre-state Israel and work the land as pioneers. Before World War II, there were 70,000 Hashomer Hatzair members worldwide and many of those in Nazi-occupied territories led resistance activities in the ghettos and concentration camps or joined partisan groups in the forests of east-central Europe. It is the oldest Zionist youth movement still in existence. *See also* Zionism.

Iron Guard A fascist party founded in 1927, later known as the Legion or the Legionary Movement, that was based on Romanian nationalism and antisemitism. Its political influence spanned from 1930 to 1941, when it was crushed by Ion Antonescu. *See also* Antonescu, Legionnaires.

Kabbalah (Hebrew; receiving) The Jewish mystical tradition.

Kaddish (Aramaic; holy) Also known as the Mourner's Prayer, Kaddish is said as part of mourning rituals in Jewish prayer services as well as at funerals and memorials.

Kindertransport (German; literally, children's transport) The organized attempts by British and American groups to get Jewish children out of Nazi Germany. Between December 1938 and September 3, 1939, the government-sanctioned but privately funded Kindertransport rescued nearly 10,000 children under the age of seventeen and placed them in British foster homes and hostels.

kippot (Hebrew; plural of *kippah*) A skullcap or small head covering worn by Jewish men as a sign of reverence for God.

Legionnaires Members of the Romanian Legionary Movement or

Iron Guard, who organized boycotts of Jewish businesses and engaged in violent attacks on Jews and synagogues. *See also* Iron Guard.

Lubavitch A branch of Hasidic Judaism that was founded in Lyubavichi, Lithuania, in the late eighteenth century. The Lubavitch philosophy differs from other Hasidic branches in that it emphasizes intellectual over emotional reasoning. Members of the Lubavitch movement are involved in outreach to Jews worldwide.

maftir (Hebrew; concluder) Refers to both the last person called up to read the Torah as well as to the Torah portion that is read.

mensch (Yiddish) A good, decent person, someone having honourable qualities; *mensch* generally refers to someone who is selfless or who has integrity.

mikvah (Hebrew; literally, a pool or gathering of water) A ritual purification bath taken by Jews on occasions that denote change in time, such as before the Sabbath (signifying the shift from a regular weekday to a holy day of rest), or in personal status, such as before a person's wedding or, for a married woman, after menstruation. The word mikvah refers to both the pool of water and the building that houses the ritual bath.

Orthodox Judaism The set of beliefs and practices of Jews for whom the observance of Jewish law is closely connected to faith; it is characterized by strict religious observance of Jewish dietary laws, restrictions on work on the Sabbath and holidays, and a code of modesty in dress.

partisans Members of irregular military forces or resistance movements formed to oppose armies of occupation. During World War II there were a number of different partisan groups that opposed both the Nazis and their collaborators in several countries. The term partisan could include highly organized, almost paramilitary groups such as the Red Army partisans; ad hoc groups bent more on survival than resistance; and roving groups of bandits who plundered what they could from all sides during the war.

Rabbi Judah Loew ben Bezalel (1520–1609) Also known as the Maharal (a Hebrew acronym for a phrase meaning "our teacher, the rabbi Loew") of Prague, Loew was a prominent Talmudic scholar, philosopher and mystic. It is claimed that Loew created a Golem, a being of clay, to protect and defend the Jews of Prague from antisemitic attacks. He led congregations in the cities of Mikulov and Prague.

Red Cross A humanitarian organization founded in 1863 to protect the victims of war. During World War II the Red Cross provided assistance to prisoners of war by distributing food parcels and monitoring the situation in POW camps, and also provided medical attention to wounded soldiers and civilians. Today, in addition to the international body, the International Committee of the Red Cross (ICRC), there are national Red Cross and Red Crescent societies in almost every country in the world.

Satmar Rebbe Rabbi Joel Teitelbaum (1887–1979), who founded a strictly Orthodox Jewish and anti-Zionist movement while living in the town of Satmar, Hungary. The movement continues to have thousands of members across North America and Europe.

Sephardi (Hebrew) The adjective used to describe Sephardim, Jews of Spanish, Portuguese or North-African descent. The word derives from the biblical name for a country that is taken to be Spain.

Shabbat (Hebrew; in Yiddish, Shabbes, Shabbos; in English, Sabbath) The weekly day of rest beginning Friday at sunset and ending Saturday at nightfall, ushered in by the lighting of candles on Friday evening and the recitation of blessings over wine and challah (egg bread); a day of celebration as well as prayer, it is customary to eat three festive meals, attend synagogue services and refrain from doing any work or travelling.

sheitl (Yiddish; wig) A head covering worn by Orthodox Jewish women to abide by religious codes of modesty.

shiva (Hebrew; literally, seven) In Judaism, the seven-day mourning period that is observed after the funeral of a close relative.

shul (Yiddish) Synagogue or Jewish house of prayer.

Spielberg, Steven (1946–) An American film director who founded the Survivors of the Shoah Visual History Foundation in 1994, as a result of his experience making the film *Schindler's List. See also* Survivors of the Shoah Visual History Foundation.

SS (abbreviation of Schutzstaffel; Defence Corps). The SS was established in 1925 as Adolf Hitler's elite corps of personal bodyguards. Under the direction of Heinrich Himmler, its membership grew from 280 in 1929 to 50,000 when the Nazis came to power in 1933, and to nearly a quarter of a million on the eve of World War II. The SS was comprised of the Allgemeine-SS (General SS) and the Waffen-SS (Armed, or Combat SS). The General SS dealt with policing and the enforcement of Nazi racial policies in Germany and the Nazi-occupied countries.

Stalin, Joseph (1878–1953) The leader of the Soviet Union from 1924 until his death in 1953. Born Joseph Vissarionovich Dzhugashvili, he changed his name to Stalin (literally: man of steel) in 1903. He was a staunch supporter of Lenin, taking control of the Communist Party upon Lenin's death. Very soon after acquiring leadership of the Communist Party, Stalin ousted rivals, killed opponents in purges, and effectively established himself as a dictator. During the late 1930s, Stalin commenced "The Great Purge," during which he targeted and disposed of elements within the Communist Party that he deemed to be a threat to the stability of the Soviet Union. These purges extended to both military and civilian society, and millions of people were incarcerated or exiled to harsh labour camps. During the war and in the immediate postwar period, many Jews in Poland viewed Stalin as the leader of the country that liberated them and saved them from death at the hands of the Nazis. At the time, many people were unaware of the extent of Stalin's own murderous policies. After World War II, Stalin set up Communist governments controlled by Moscow in many Eastern European states bordering and close to the USSR, and instituted antisemitic campaigns and purges.

Star of David (in Hebrew, *Magen David*) The six-pointed star that is the ancient and most recognizable symbol of Judaism. During World War II, Jews in Nazi-occupied areas were frequently forced to wear a badge or armband with the Star of David on it as an identifying mark of their lesser status and to single them out as targets for persecution.

Sukkot (Hebrew; Feast of Tabernacles) Autumn harvest festival that recalls the forty years during which the ancient Israelites wandered the desert after their exodus from slavery in Egypt. The holiday lasts for seven days, during which Jews traditionally eat meals in a sukkah, a small structure covered with a roof made from leaves or branches.

Survivors of the Shoah Visual History Foundation A project founded by Steven Spielberg in 1994 as a result of his experience making the film *Schindler's List*. The foundation's mission is to record and preserve the testimonies of Holocaust survivors in a video archive and to promote Holocaust education. In 2006, after recording about 52,000 international testimonies, the foundation partnered with the University of Southern California and became the USC Shoah Foundation Institute for Visual History and Education.

talleisim (Yiddish; plural of *tallis*) Jewish prayer shawl traditionally worn during morning prayers and on the Day of Atonement (Yom Kippur). One usually wears the *tallis* over one's shoulders but some choose to place it over their heads to express awe in the presence of God.

Ten Lost Tribes A term referring to the ten tribes of the Kingdom of Israel who were conquered and exiled by the Assyrians in 722 BCE. Many legends exist as to what happened to the tribes, with different groups claiming to be descended from them.

Torah (Hebrew) The Five Books of Moses (the first five books of the Bible), also called the Pentateuch. The Torah is the core of Jewish scripture, traditionally believed to have been given to Moses on

Mount Sinai. In Christianity it is referred to as the "Old Testament."

Transnistria A 16,000-square-mile region between the Dniester and Bug rivers that originally had been part of Ukraine. After German and Romanian forces conquered Ukraine in the summer of 1941, Romania administered this territory and deported hundreds of thousands of Jews there, where many were killed or died of illness and starvation.

ulpan (Hebrew; plural *ulpanim*) A school that offers an intensive Hebrew-language study program. *Ulpanim*, the first of which was established in Jerusalem in 1949, were created to help new immigrants learn the language of their new country and acclimatize to its culture.

Union of Communist Youth A wing of Romania's Communist Party, established in 1922 to involve young people in the movement's political activities.

Western Wall (also Wailing Wall; in Hebrew, Kotel; literally, wall) A remnant of a wall from the second Jewish Temple built by Herod the Great in Jerusalem, constructed in 19 BCE. It is considered the most sacred site in Judaism.

Yiddish A language derived from Middle High German with elements of Hebrew, Aramaic, Romance and Slavic languages, and written in Hebrew characters. Spoken by Jews in east-central Europe for roughly a thousand years from the tenth century to the mid-twentieth century, it was still the most common language among European Jews until the outbreak of World War II.

Yom Kippur (Hebrew; literally, Day of Atonement) A solemn day of fasting and repentance that comes eight days after Rosh Hashanah, the Jewish New Year, and marks the end of the high holidays. Erev (first night of) Yom Kippur marks the beginning of the holiday.

Zionism A movement promoted by the Viennese Jewish journalist Theodor Herzl, who argued in his 1896 book *Der Judenstaat* (The

Jewish State) that the best way to resolve the problem of antisemi-tism and persecution of Jews in Europe was to create an inde-pendent Jewish state in the historic Jewish homeland of Biblical Israel. Zionists also promoted the revival of Hebrew as a Jewish national language.

Photographs

1 The Siegler family in pre-war Dorna. In the middle row (left to right) are Felicia's
   mother, Laura; her grandmother, Rebecca (Rivka), and other maternal relatives.
   Seated in front are Felicia's aunts Sidi (left) and Mila (right). Dorna, circa 1920.
2 Felicia's mother, Laura, with her mother and her siblings. From left to right:
   Sidi (age fourteen); Laura (age seventeen); Mila (age twelve); and their mother,
   Rebecca. Dorna, 1926.

Engagement photo of Felicia's parents, Isaac Steigman and Laura Siegler. Dorna, 1928.

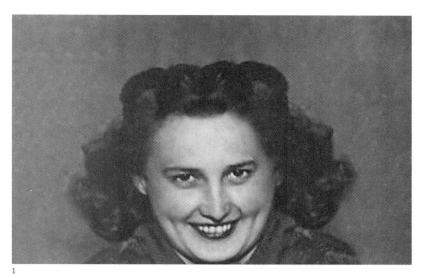

1 & 2 Felicia's aunt Etty (née Steigman) and uncle Molly Shufer.

1 Six-month-old Felicia with her maternal grandmother, Rebecca Siegler. Dorna, 1932.

2 Felicia with her mother and her mother's cousin under a banner reading "The Road of Life." Dorna, circa 1937.

1

2

1 Felicia, age six, with her mother. Dorna, 1937.
2 Felicia and her family in Dorna's park. Left to right: Felicia's maternal grandmother, Rebecca; Felicia's father, Isaac; Aunt Mila; Felicia; and Felicia's mother,
   Laura. Dorna, 1937.

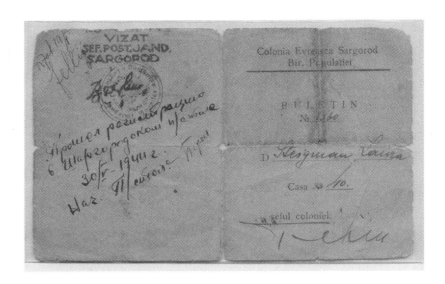

Laura Steigman's ID card. Shargorod, 1944.

1

2

1 The only wartime photo available of Felicia (far right) in Shargorod. Felicia is pictured with her teacher, Madame Victor (centre), and four classmates – Hedy, Paula, Selma and Renate. Shargorod, Transnistria, 1941.

2 Felicia (far left) after the war with her father, grandmother and mother. Dorna, 1948.

1 Felicia (middle row, seated) with her Socialist-Zionist group after the war, visiting a sheep shelter in the Carpathian Mountains.

2 Felicia (third from right), with friends in front of the building she arranged to have used as a high school. Dorna, 1946.

Aunt Sidi with the Treiser family, who Felicia was close to in Montreal. Standing in back: Felicia's uncle Armin Treiser and aunt Sidi Rauchwerger. In front: Felicia's aunt Mila Treiser with her children, Murray and Diana. Montreal, 1958.

1 Felicia's daughter, Romy, age four, at the wedding of Diana Treiser and Israel Kogan. Montreal, 1969.
2 Romy with her grandmother, Laura Steigman. Montreal, circa 1969.
3 Felicia's parents in Montreal, circa 1960s.

1   The names of Felicia's cousins Charna Mauler and Anna Pachter, and of her paternal grandmother, Beile Steigman, are shown on the back of an unidentified family member's monument in the Jewish cemetery in Dorna. The names of family members who died in the Holocaust and therefore had no graves were often engraved on the back of another family member's gravestone.

2   Gravesite of Sidi Rauchwerger, who died in Israel.

3   Felicia's father's gravestone in Israel.

4   Gravestone of Felicia's mother, Toronto.

1 Felicia Carmelly. Toronto, 1981.
2 Felicia facilitating a stress management seminar. Toronto, circa 1983.

The cover of Felicia's book, *Shattered!*, published in 1997.

Felicia (second from left) at her book launch with the Romanian consul (left); the consul's wife (third from left); and Manuel Prutschi (right), of the now-defunct Canadian Jewish Congress. Toronto, 1997.

1 Bill and Felicia with the Treiser and Kogan families at Adam Treiser's bar mitzvah
  in New York. Left to right: Matthew Treiser; Bill; Felicia; Adam Treiser; Murray
  Treiser; and Diana and Israel Kogan.
2 Wedding of Jenevieve and Matthew Treiser, son of Felicia's cousin Murray Treiser.
  From left to right: Felicia, Bill, Robin, Murray, Cameron, Matthew, Jenevieve,
  Mila (in front), Adam, Diana, Israel and Jessica.

1 The children, grandchildren and great-grandchildren of Molly and Etty (Steigman) Shufer, from Felicia's father's side of the family. From left to right: Yael (with Ilai behind her); Amit; Ofra; Avital; Daniel (in front); Avital; Uriah; Tzila, Ya'akov's wife; Ya'akov Shofar, eldest son of Etty and Molly; Rafael; Alon; Asaf; and Yoav. Israel, circa 2012. (Not pictured: The younger son of Etty and Molly, Yuval Shofar, who has a high rank in the Israel Defense Forces.)

2 Felicia's daughter, Romy, with her husband, Richard Fine. Toronto, circa 2011.

Felicia and Bill.

Index

The Azrieli Foundation

The Azrieli Foundation was established in 1989 to realize and extend the philanthropic vision of David J. Azrieli, C.M., C.Q., M.Arch. The Foundation's mission is to support a wide spectrum of initiatives in education and research. The Azrieli Foundation is an active supporter of programs in the fields of Education, the education of architects, scientific and medical research, and the arts. The Azrieli Foundation's many initiatives include: the Holocaust Survivor Memoirs Program, which collects, preserves, publishes and distributes the written memoirs of survivors in Canada; the Azrieli Institute for Educational Empowerment, an innovative program successfully working to keep at-risk youth in school; the Azrieli Fellows Program, which promotes academic excellence and leadership on the graduate level at Israeli universities; the Azrieli Music Project, which celebrates and fosters the creation of high-quality new Jewish orchestral music; and the Azrieli Neurodevelopmental Research Program, which supports advanced research on neurodevelopmental disorders, particularly Fragile X and Autism Spectrum Disorders.